AIDS in Africa

AIDS IN AFRICA

How the Poor are Dying

Nana K. Poku

polity

First published in 2005 by Polity Press

Polity Press
65 Bridge Street
Cambridge CB2 1UR, UK

Polity Press
350 Main Street
Malden, MA 02148, USA

ISBN: 0-7456-3158-4
ISBN: 0-7456-3159-2 (pb)

A catalogue record for this book is available from the British
Library.

Typeset in 11 on 13 pt Berling
by SNP Best-set Typesetter Ltd, Hong Kong
Printed and bound in India by
Replika Press Pvt. Ltd

The publisher has used its best endeavours to ensure that the URLs
for external websites referred to in this book are correct and active
at the time of going to press. However, the publisher has no
responsibility for the websites and can make no guarantee that a site
will remain live or that the content is or will remain appropriate.

Every effort has been made to trace all copyright holders, but if any
have been inadvertently overlooked the publishers will be pleased to
include any necessary credits in any subsequent reprint or edition.

For further information on Polity, visit our website: www.polity.co.uk

Contents

Figures, Tables and Boxes

Figures

Tables

Boxes

Acronyms and Abbreviations

AIDS	Acquired Immune Deficiency Syndrome
AMREF	African Medical & Research Foundation
ART	antiretroviral therapy
ARVs	antiretrovirals
BIDPA	Botswana Institute for Development Policy Analysis
CBOs	community-based organizations
CDC	Centres for Disease Control and Prevention
CHGA	Commission on HIV/AIDS and Governance in Africa
COPE	Community-Oriented Primary Education
CRFs	circulating recombinant forms
EFA	Education For All
ESAF	Enhanced Structural Adjustment Facility
FAO	Food and Agriculture Organization of the United Nations
FBOs	faith-based organizations
FDI	foreign direct investment
FIDA	International Federation of Women Lawyers
FOCUS	Families, Orphans and Children Under Stress
GDP	gross domestic product
GNP	gross national product
HAG	Health Rights Action Group

HDI	Human Development Index
HEPS	Coalition for Health Promotion and Social Development
HIPC	Heavily Indebted Poor Countries
HIV	Human Immunodeficiency Virus
IECs	information and education campaigns
IGAs	income-generating activities
ILO	International Labour Organization
IMF	International Monetary Fund
MAP	Multi-country HIV/AIDS Programme
MDG	Millennium Development Goal
MSF	Médécins sans Frontières
MTCT	mother-to-child transmission
MTP	Medium Term Plan
NACWOLA	National Community of Women Living with HIV/AIDS
NGO	non-governmental organization
NSP	National Strategic Plan
OECD	Organization for Economic Co-operation and Development
OIs	opportunistic infections
OPEC	Organization of Petroleum-Exporting Countries
PEPFAR	President's Emergency Plan for AIDS Relief
PLWHA	people living with HIV and AIDS
PRGF	Poverty Reduction and Growth Facility
SAPs	structural adjustment programmes
STDs	sexually transmitted diseases
STIs	sexually transmitted infections
TASO	The AIDS Support Organization
TB	tuberculosis
UN	United Nations
UNAIDS	Joint United Nations Programme on HIV/AIDS
UNDP	United Nations Development Programme
UNGASS	United Nations General Assembly Special Session on AIDS

UNICEF	United Nations Children's Fund
VCT	voluntary counselling and testing
WDI	World Development Indicators
WHO	World Health Organization
YONECO	Youth Net and Counselling

Acknowledgements

The writing of this book was made possible because of the hard work and support of Bjorg Sandkjaer and Ingvild Oia, both of whom provided key research support for each of the chapters in the book. I am indebted to Polity Press, particularly David Held and Ellen McKinlay for their encouragement to publish this book. Justin Dyer provided excellent editorial support to ensure that the manuscript was in the best shape it could be. I am also grateful to the anonymous reviewer of the manuscript for the insightful comments offered, which were profoundly helpful in guiding me through redrafts of sections of the book.

This book is dedicated to Milly Katana, lobbyist, activist and a source of tremendous inspiration.

Introduction: Africa's AIDS Crisis in Context

No reason yet exists to suggest that the HIV epidemic is significantly slowing down anywhere in Africa. Each day of continuing spread adds to the ramifications and duration of its devastating impact. The statistics on the toll that the epidemic has already exacted paint a grim picture, as do the forecasts of the consequences which are still anticipated to unfold over the medium to long term. Communities across the continent are experiencing a day-to-day decline in their standards of living, reduced capacities for personal and social achievements, an increasingly uncertain future, and a diminished capacity to maintain what has been secured over past decades in terms of social and economic development (Poku and Whiteside, 2004). As a result, a true process of immiseration is now observable in many parts of the continent – particularly southern Africa (Mutangadura, 2000; Whiteside and Sunter, 2000).

Like all events on such a scale, the impact of HIV/AIDS on Africa ranges far beyond the harrowing catalogue of lives lost, into the prosperity or poverty of nations, the character of government and the fabric of social and community life. In this sense, the epidemic could be seen as a survival issue for Africa. Not only does it spell an early and painful death for millions of individuals, it also threatens to derail the continent's prospects for development.

Though many who study the dynamics of the epidemic will readily concede that, in some sense, its entrenchment is a socially produced phenomenon, few have examined how the course, direction and impacts of the epidemic have been affected by the continent's ubiquitous poverty, the pervasive prescriptions from international financial agencies or Africa's marginalization in the globalization process. Moreover, few analysts have attempted, systematically, to map and assess the likely ramifications of the epidemic for the ability of political and social structures to function normally in the years to come. Considering, however, the gravity of the epidemic and the devastating human resource losses it entails, understanding its implications for political stability and economic development demands our immediate attention.

While the idea that health is influenced by political and economic forces is not new, the actual practice of documenting these connections remains rare. This is particularly true of Africa's HIV/AIDS epidemic, which has largely been seen as a public health crisis, rather than a developmental crisis of perhaps biblical proportions. It is with this task that this book is primarily concerned. Using primary and secondary data, it seeks to unpack the socio-economic context of vulnerability to HIV/AIDS as well as the politics of mitigation and response – both domestic and global. It focuses on the environment rather than on individual psychology or behaviour in constructing a series of arguments designed to chart the dominant forces driving the epidemic, frustrating the possibility of alleviation and recovery as well as working to relegate Africa to a bleak and vulnerable future.

The Poverty–Vulnerability Nexus and 'Mbeki's Temerity'

What I have heard is that extreme poverty is the world's biggest killer and the greatest cause of ill health and suffering across the globe. I have heard stories being told about malaria, tuberculosis, hepatitis B, HIV-AIDS and other diseases. As I listened even longer to this tale of human woe, I heard the name recur with frightening frequency – Africa, Africa, Africa. In the end, I have come to the conclusion that as Africans, we are confronted by a health crisis of enormous proportions. One of the consequences of this crisis is the deeply disturbing phenomenon of the collapse of immune systems among millions of our people, such that their bodies have no natural defence against attack by many viruses and bacteria. As I listened and heard the whole story told about our own country, it seemed to me that we could not blame everything on a single virus. The world's biggest killer and the greatest cause of ill health and suffering across the globe, including South Africa, is extreme poverty.

This contextualization of Africa's HIV/AIDS crisis in the continent's ubiquitous poverty caused a tremendous political storm when President Thabo Mbeki suggested it at the opening address of the 13th International AIDS conference in Durban, South Africa, in June 2000. Mbeki's 'temerity', as one Western scientist viewed it, was to challenge the established view that Africa's HIV crisis was functionally related to its unusually high rates of sexual partner change and the nature of sexual politics more broadly on the continent. Dr Yuichi Shiokawa from the University of Tokyo put the position this way: 'the AIDS crisis in Africa could be brought under control only if Africans restrained their sexual cravings.' Notwithstanding the fact that there is no empirical evidence to support this view, the central thrust of prevention programmes over the past two decades has been dominated by the advocacy of behavioural modification and the encouragement of condom use.

But how much sex are we talking about that would produce, in the absence of other factors, prevalence of HIV in Botswana that is over fifty times that of the United States, eighty times that of France and 1,000 times that of Cuba? Clearly, sexual behaviour is an important factor in the transmission of sexually transmitted diseases (Stillwagon, 2001). But sexual behaviour alone cannot explain HIV prevalence as high as 25 per cent of the adult population in some African countries and less than 1 per cent in the developed world. In truth, the answer to the question posed above lies as much in the context of the disease as the behaviour of the people concerned. The environment in which any infection is transmitted in poor countries is very different from that of the rich countries. In the former, it is strongly influenced by poverty, malnutrition, bad water and poor access to preventive and curative care.

In this sense it is possible that at the Durban conference, President Mbeki's proposition was neither unsuitable nor irrational. It seems to be echoing Louis Pasteur's comment that 'the microbe is nothing, the terrain everything' (Jakab, 2000, p. 1). This is a view also shared by the late Jonathan Mann (who became the founding director of the WHO's Global Programme on AIDS) when he concluded that 'those people who were marginalized, stigmatized and discriminated against – before HIV/AIDS arrived – have later become, over time, those at highest risk of HIV infection' (Mann, 1999, p. 15). For Pasteur and Mann, the environment in which any infection is transmitted is bound to be strongly influenced by crucial societal factors such as the levels of poverty, sanitation, malnutrition, bad water and access to preventive and curative care. In other words, pre-existing health conditions play a key role in people's susceptibility to any disease.

To be clear, what is in contention is not that everything President Mbeki has uttered on this subject of HIV/AIDS is right; nor, indeed, can one deny that there is considerable merit in the argument that particular societal factors are exposing Africans to a greater risk of contracting the HIV virus. In truth, some of President Mbeki's recent comments questioning the link between HIV and AIDS have been irresponsible, not least because they fly in the face of scientific wisdom, while inadvertently fuelling a denialist movement at a time when political leadership is needed across the continent to mount an effective and sustained response against the epidemic.

This notwithstanding, there is much merit in calling for a greater contextualization of the epidemic. The following paragraph from an interview in South Africa dramatizes the complex interconnectivity of poverty and vulnerability to disease:

> My husband lost his job about five months ago. It was a big shock but we thought we could cope. I was earning a reasonably good wage. We had to cut a few corners though. We had to eat less meat. We had to save on all kinds of things. . . . Then two months ago I lost my job. We were desperate. There was no money coming in now. . . . Now they've cut off the electricity and we're two months in arrears with rent. They're going to evict us, I'm sure, we just can't pay though. My husband decided to go to Jo'burg. . . . I don't know where he is. . . . Sometimes [the children] lie awake at night crying. I know they are crying because they are hungry. I feel like feeding them Rattex [rat poison]. When your children cry hunger crying, your heart wants to break. It will be better if they were dead. When I think things like that I feel worse. . . . I'm sick. I'm sick because of the cold. I can't take my children to the doctor when they are sick because there is no money. . . . What can one do? You must start looking. You can also pray to God that he will keep you from killing your children. ('Zuki' 2003)

This woman's experience shows the innumerable mechanisms through which poverty creates a milieu of risk. She knows, even without necessarily being in possession of the relevant statistics, that poverty is closely linked with high unemployment, hunger and malnutrition, lack of basic services, inability to pay for or access health care, disintegration of families, vulnerability, homelessness and often hopelessness. We might remind ourselves at this stage that in the absence of penicillin, the war-ravaged Europe of the late 1940s would have been devastated by epidemics of syphilis and gonorrhoea. That threat was the natural outcome of the concomitance of societal forces; chief among these was the devastating impact of war, the associated poverty, men without social constraints and women without any means of support for themselves and their families except prostitution or something close to it.

Mainstream biomedical and social scientific literature has long documented the methods by which this combination of factors can undermine the body's specific and non-specific immune response (Farmer et al., 1996; Jakab, 2000; McNeill, 1998). Hence, we know that protein-energy malnutrition (general calorie deficit) and specific micronutrient deficiencies, such as vitamin-A deficiency, weaken every part of the body's immune system, including the skin and mucous membranes, which are particularly important in protecting the body from sexually transmitted diseases, including HIV (Kim et al., 2000; Farmer, 1999). Moreover, in an environment of poverty, parasite infestation plays a dual role in suppressing immune response. It aggravates malnutrition by robbing the body of essential nutrients and increasing calorie demand. In addition, the presence of parasites chronically triggers the immune system, impairing its ability to fight infection from other pathogens (McNeill, 1998).

One of the key legacies of poverty in Africa is the existence of undiagnosed and untreated STDs among many of the population. Data for 2003 indicate that Africa has the highest incidence of curable STDs at 284 cases per 1,000 people aged 15–49 years, compared to the second highest of 160 cases per 1,000 people in South and South-East Asia (UNAIDS, 2004b). There is now growing recognition of the public health implications of curable STDs (especially those causing genital ulcers) by virtue of their frequency of occurrence as well as their ability, when present, to facilitate the transmission of HIV (World Bank, 2000b). One study suggests that the presence of an untreated STD can increase the risk of both the acquisition and transmission of HIV by a factor of up to 10. Such painful bacterial STDs are relatively uncommon in rich countries because of the availability of antibiotics (MEDILINKS, 2001). Yet in Africa, even when the poor have access to health care, the clinics may have no antibiotics with which to treat bacterial STDs that act as co-factors for AIDS. Sub-Saharan Africa is not the only region in which malnutrition is associated with HIV/AIDS. Among all low- and middle-income countries, HIV prevalence is strongly correlated with falling protein consumption and falling calorie consumption.

Janie Simmons et al. (1996) pursue the theme further, noting that, 'through a myriad of mechanisms, it [poverty] creates an environment of risk' (p. 53). Certainly, the poor seem to represent a disproportionate amount of the number of people infected with HIV globally. Perhaps more than anywhere else, the wealthiest country in the world – the United States (in which at least 20 per cent of the people nevertheless live in poverty) – provides an important example of the role of poverty as the main driving force of the epidemic. Here, HIV has moved almost unimpeded through poor communities – mostly of colour. By the end of 2004, African Americans, who comprise approximately 12 per cent of the US population, made up more than 26 per cent of the country's poor and accounted for 37 per cent of all reported cases of HIV/AIDS.

The link between poverty and vulnerability to HIV/AIDS is brought into an even sharper focus by looking at the global distribution of infections. The glaring fact from figure 2.1 in this regard is that 95 per cent of the global distribution of HIV infections and AIDS cases are located in the developing world. Here, as elsewhere, poverty is associated with weak endowments of human and financial resources, such as low levels of education with associated low levels of literacy and few marketable skills, generally poor health status and low labour productivity. An aspect of this poor health status is the existence of undiagnosed and untreated STDs – which is now recognized as a very significant co-factor in the transmission of HIV (WHO, 2000, p. 2). Poor households typically have few – if any – financial or other assets and are often politically and socially marginalized. It is not at all surprising in these circumstances that the poor often adopt coping mechanisms which inadvertently expose them to a higher risk of contracting the HIV virus (see chapter 2).

A note of caution must be entered here because to acknowledge the synergistic relationship between poverty and vulnerability to HIV is not to conclude that AIDS itself is a nutritionally based disease. Equally, it is important not to deny that HIV is sexually transmitted across the African continent and causes AIDS. It merely suggests that any disease in Africa must be placed in the context of the continent's underdevelopment, however transmitted (see chapter 1). This is particularly important because the behavioural change hypothesis, which remains the dominant policy response to the continent's AIDS crisis, has been less than effective as it has failed to acknowledge the complex but real relationship between the continent's traditional problems and the entrenchment of the HIV/AIDS epidemic.

Take, for example, the Medium-Term Plans (MTPs) from the leading multilateral donors – mainly the International Monetary Fund (IMF) and the World Bank – which have become the central organizing structures for the design and implementation of domestic response to HIV and AIDS in many African countries. At the beginning of the epidemic, MTPs were primarily ways of organizing public health responses to the crisis. More than twenty years into the epidemic, MTPs – in their construction and in their core elements – have remained largely focused on public health concerns. This is particularly perverse given the fact that our knowledge about the epidemic's impact on the continent's fragile development capacity has been sophisticated for at least a decade (Baggaley et al., 1994; Kambou et al., 1992; Mann and Tarantola, 1992).

We have known for some time, for example, that economic need and dependency lead to activities that magnify the risk of HIV transmission and mean that many people, particularly women, are powerless to protect themselves against infection. Inequitable power structures, a lack of legal protection and inadequate standards of health and nutrition all further exacerbate the spread of the virus, accelerate progression from HIV infection to AIDS, and aggravate the plight of those affected by the epidemic. Further, the setting of the HIV epidemic in Africa creates a downward spiral whereby existing social, economic and human deprivation produces a particularly fertile environment for the spread of HIV and, in turn, the HIV epidemic compounds and intensifies the deprivation already experienced by people across the continent. In this sense, AIDS is more than a disease. It is also much more than a public health crisis. AIDS in Africa is a development crisis of historic proportions. Of course, by treating the epidemic as a health crisis caused by a hyper-sexualized culture, the World Bank and the IMF can continue to pursue their abhorrent structural adjustment programmes (SAPs) on the continent, uninterrupted (see chapter 2).

The Challenge of HIV/AIDS to Development

It follows from the discussions above that to fully understand the scale of Africa's HIV-led crisis, one must proceed from the fact that it is complex, multi-faceted and influenced by many medical, social, economic and cultural factors. Though it has much in common with other infectious diseases, it also presents relatively distinctive features. The epidemic brings three processes together in a unique and particularly devastating combination:

- First, HIV/AIDS is killing people in the prime of their working lives (typically those aged between 15 and 49). This has the effect of sharply reducing life expectancy, eroding the labour force and destroying intergenerational socio-cultural capital formation.
- Second and relatedly, by destroying intergenerational capital formation, HIV/AIDS is also weakening the ability of succeeding generations to maintain development achievements of the past.
- Third, the net effect of the preceding two processes is the systematic erosion of a state's ability to replenish the

stock and flow of vital human capital needed to sustain socio-economic development and political governance.

The combined effects of these processes are initially manifested at the level of households and communities – see chapter 3. For governments, the unfolding immiseration of families and communities resulting from the impact of HIV/AIDS poses a number of challenges to socio-economic development. One such challenge is the threat of worsening social inequality (see chapter 3). This is particular pertinent in relation to the increasing number of orphans being created by HIV/AIDS. As was noted earlier, AIDS selectively destroys human capital, that is, people's accumulated life experiences, their human and job skills, and their knowledge and insights built up over a period of years or generations. If one or, worse, both parents die while their children are still young, the transmission of knowledge and potential productive capacity across the two generations becomes severely weakened. At the same time, the loss of income due to disability and early death reduces the lifetime resources available to the family, which may well result in the children spending much less time (if any at all) at school.

If the children left orphaned are not given the care and education enjoyed by those whose parents remain uninfected, the potential for increased inequality among the next generation of young adults and the families they form is increased considerably. Moreover, social customs of adoption and fostering, however well established, are proving insufficient to cope with the scale of the problem generated by a sharp increase in adult mortality. This is compounded by the fact that extended family systems are fragmenting because of changes in social patterns and the impact of the epidemic itself.

The macro-economic costs of AIDS impose an extra burden on already poor and vulnerable economies. Although the headline figure of GDP impact is low – between 0.4 and 1.5 per cent reduction in annual growth according to most studies (see table 3.4) – this conceals more profound effects on society and government capacity. As the sickness strikes at the labour force, it takes a toll on productivity, profitability, investment, savings and, ultimately, government's ability to function normally. In the case of the small kingdom of Swaziland, for example, the Ministry of Finance, the Ministry of Economic Planning and Development and the Ministry of Public Services and Information are expected to collectively lose 32 per cent of the workforce to HIV/AIDS over the next decade. All three agencies will need to replace an additional 1.6 per cent of the staff complement each year to maintain the current level of staffing over the same period. Similarly, in Malawi, an average of 2.3 per cent of staff were lost to HIV/AIDS each year from five public sector institutions between 1990 and 2000. These human losses were taking place against a background of only 0.7 per cent recruitment per year within the same institutions.

Therefore, the cumulative effects of HIV/AIDS mean that essential services may grind to a halt, while livelihoods and social protection collapse, and poverty and hunger escalate. If the epidemic rages unchecked, the continent faces a spiral of decline, with huge implications for political governance for succeeding generations. Already, HIV/AIDS is creating a downward spiral whereby existing social, economic and human deprivation is producing a particularly fertile environment for the spread of the virus and, in turn, the epidemic is also compounding and intensifying the deprivation already experienced by the people on the continent. The process is thus insidious, since the full effects will be felt only over the long term, as increasing mortality among the most economically active members of African societies translates into low adult productivity a generation or two later. The net effect of an AIDS-depleted society is a challenge to development resulting from the potential-hollowed states and social networks. For these reasons, HIV/AIDS may well pose the gravest threat to socio-political and -economic development in Africa.

The cruel irony, of course, is that Africa is the least equipped region in the world to deal with the multiplicity of challenges posed by HIV/AIDS. Despite two decades of SAPs, the promised advantages of economic restructuring, as hailed by the various lending bodies, have not materialized in Africa. Foreign investments have failed to flow in, the debt burdens have mounted and commodity prices continue to fluctuate amid declining industries. Not surprisingly, poverty has been increasing at a faster rate than anywhere else in the world, such that Africans account for one in four poor people in the world (World Bank 2000a, p. 3). Amid this depressing picture of retrogression and decline, new evidence suggests that HIV is eroding the continent's already fragile development capacity. In many parts of eastern, central and southern Africa, HIV/AIDS means that governments, the private sector, communities and households now face the day-to-day experience of falling standards of living, reduced capacities for personal and social achievement, worsening expectations of what the future holds (with important consequences for what can be achieved today) and a diminished capacity to maintain what has been secured over past decades in terms of social and economic development (Poku, 2001).

Structure of the Book

This book is a contribution to an emerging literature which seeks to place the continent's struggle against HIV/AIDS, including responses to it, within the broader framework of its development challenges (see Poku and Whiteside, 2004). The book brings together relevant data and information and presents the material in ways that are non-technical and easily accessible to lay readers. The intention is to reach policy makers and other stakeholders with easily accessible information on the HIV epidemic, and to ensure that they understand the complex interactions between development objectives (e.g. the Millennium Development Goals [MDGs]) and the impact of HIV/AIDS. The case is made through a presentation of data (charts especially, together with brief case studies) that is visually dramatic in terms of the impact of HIV/AIDS on children, adult mortality, life expectancy, human resources, the productive sectors, and so on.

The book consist of six chapters: chapter 1 deals with the socio-economic determinants of vulnerability, by focusing on Africa's post-colonial economic decline and its resultant implications for poverty trends and the health outcomes of people on the continent. The chapter examines the role of political elites, international organizations and global economic forces in shaping the continent's recent socio-economic history. In so doing, it provides the reader with a clear appreciation of why Africa has been so vulnerable to the HIV/AIDS epidemic.

The second chapter examines some of the core drivers of the epidemic in Africa as well as demystifying some of the dominant myths about the HIV virus. In order to understand the scale of Africa's HIV-led crisis, one must proceed from the fact that it is complex, multi-faceted and influenced by many medical, social, economic and cultural factors. Though it has much in common with other infectious diseases, it also presents relatively unusual features. As a result of this complexity there is a great deal of misinformation that needs to be clarified before we move on to some of the key challenges posed by it to societies and communities across the African continent; it is with this task that the chapter is primarily concerned.

Chapter 3 makes the case for why HIV/AIDS poses the greatest challenge to continuing development in Africa. It argues that AIDS death brings with it loss of productive resources through the sale of livestock to pay for sickness, mourning and funeral expenses, as well as a sharp decline in productivity. Sickness also contributes to the scarcity of labour because of both the incapacity of workers and the time others have to devote to looking after them. The net effect of these losses on households, communities and the economic trajectory of countries is examined in this chapter. A core conclusion of the chapter is that HIV/AIDS is reshaping the demographic structure of communities, diminishing the capacity of states for sustainable development while simultaneously reducing their ability to maintain what has been secured over past decades in terms of social and economic growth.

Chapter 4 makes an unapologetic case for scaling up treatment and care programmes as the most effective mitigation strategy against the adverse impacts of the epidemic. The chapter argues that for the first time in the history of AIDS in Africa, despair over unmitigated mass human suffering is giving way to hope over the possibility of feasible AIDS care in the form of increasing access to antiretroviral medication (ARVs). Yet the evidence base for effective action in Africa is meagre. Indiscriminate drug use, ineffective care and lack of trained personnel are all real threats on a continent without a strong health care infrastructure or a regulatory environment. In the African context of limited resources and huge unmet demands for HIV care, efficient programmes clearly necessitate that mitigation strategies be properly delivered through organized channels which imply a strong involvement of governments. Using primary data, the chapter sets out to explain how treatment might be scaled up and sustained in Africa.

Chapter 5 is devoted to highlighting the role that civil society organizations are playing to provide support for people living with HIV and AIDS (PLWHA) within their communities across the continent. A central argument of the chapter is that interventional strategies need to be rooted in community responses, both to understand the impact of the epidemic and to change their individual and organizational approaches to support community action. This means developing a culture of facilitation rather than intervention. The role of facilitation is to build horizontal linkages, create opportunities for learning from local action, and foster a constructive and supportive environment. This will ensure the efficacy of intervention strategies.

The final chapter explains the challenges ahead by calling for greater political, economic and institutional leadership from policy makers to address the whole range of challenges posed by the epidemic in Africa. I seek to explain how this might be achieved through greater partnership, between national governments, non-governmental organizations (NGOs) and the donor community. In the process, I call for greater harmonization of activities to minimize duplications; greater financial commitments to ensure the sustainability of current programmes; and greater political leadership to confront stigma and discrimination.

1
Stagnation, Decline and Vulnerability: A Brief History of Post-colonial Africa

Introduction

As noted in the introduction, in an Africa entering its third decade of adjustment pressures, the promised advantages of economic restructuring – as hailed by the various lending bodies – have not materialized. If we remove territorial boundaries from our cognitive map, we are left with a harrowing picture of societies across the continent attempting to pursue basic livelihoods within the hostile and unpredictable environment of violence, disease and corruption, as governments and state managers either fail to, or appear unable to, pursue policies which will increase the life chances of their citizens. Any account of Africa's condition must attempt to unravel what is cause and what is effect. It is precisely at the level of interpretation, however, that one must be careful not to resort to simplistic causalities or reduce its plight to a series of causal or tautological clichés, some of which often carry distinct racist connotations.

Clearly, decades of domestic economic and political mismanagement with its associated corruption, violence and resultant indebtedness cannot be overlooked. Neither can the role of colonialism, external forces and the continent's incorporation into the global political economy. In what follows, I discuss how these factors have conflated to reduce Africa to such a vulnerable state. In the process, I will argue that it is in the context of the continent's socio-economic decline that one can make sense of its disproportionate vulnerability to HIV/AIDS. For the sake of convenience, the discussion is organized under three broad themes: colonialism and its legacy for post-colonial governance; domestic socio-political and economic mismanagement; and the role of external forces. A word of caution, however, must be entered here because the evidence is quite mixed with respect to the extent to which each of these groups of factors contributes to Africa's plight.

Colonialism and Its Legacy for Post-colonial Governance

The history of the past two centuries has been marked at one and the same time by the impact of the West on Asia and Africa and by the revolt of Asia and Africa against the West. The impact was the result, above all else, of Western science and technology, which, having transformed Western societies, began at an increasing rate to have the same disruptive and creative effects on societies in other continents. The revolt was a reaction against imperialism, which reached its peak in the fourth quarter of the nineteenth century. Motivated by a mix of economic and geo-political considerations, at the conference of Berlin in 1884, European leaders finally decided the rules for the partitioning of the last great land-mass, Africa. For the Europeans it became a gigantic 'Risk' game, played with real people and real land. Zanzibar was traded for Heligoland, parts of Northern Nigeria were exchanged for fishing rights off Newfoundland, Cameroun became Kamerun for a 'free hand in Morocco'. Only 10 per cent of the continent was under direct European control in 1870, but by the end of the century only 10 per cent remained outside it. From the ownership of a landholding through a hierarchy of political administrative areas such as the community, county, state and nation, all pieces fitted together with neither overlap nor extension.

When the twentieth century opened, European power in Asia and Africa stood at its zenith; no nation, it seemed, could withstand the superiority of European arms and commerce. Today, only the vestiges of European domination remain in the former colonial worlds. Between 1945 and 1960, no less than forty countries with a combined population of eight hundred million revolted against colonialism and won their independence. Never before in the whole of human history has so revolutionary a reversal occurred with such rapidity, but it came at a huge price for countries on the African continent, particularly south of the Sahara desert. The achievement of independence by Ghana in 1957 and Guinea in 1958 came quickly and was for many observers unexpected. With very few exceptions, the dominant colonial powers (primarily the British, French and Belgian) had granted independence to their colonies by 1966. Independence therefore was not the culmination of a long process of preparation in which the end was long known and the means were carefully developed.

The whole colonial system functioned on the conviction that the administrators (the white Europeans) were sovereign; that their subjects neither understood nor wanted self-government or independence. If there was any training and adoption of the native, it was a schooling in the bureaucratic toils of colonial government; a preparation not for independence but against it. It could not be otherwise. Colonialism was based on authoritarian command; as such, it was incompatible with any preparation for self-government. In that sense, every success of administration was a failure of government. With good reason, then, both Africans and Europeans usually approached problems of governance circumspectly.

Among the colonizing powers, only the British and French made attempts to leave to Africans the administration and executive skills requisite for governing new states, but this came very late in the process. Furthermore, decisions allowing Africans the possibility of more participation in voting for legislative councils with relatively significant powers came almost entirely after independence. As a result, the real political inheritance of African states at independence was the authoritarian structures of the colonial state, an accompanying political culture and an environment of politically relevant circumstances tied heavily to the nature of colonial rule.

Under these circumstances, power did not rest in the legitimacy of public confidence and acceptance; instead, it lay firmly with the political authorities. This had a profound impact on the nature of political ideas after independence. Future African leaders, continuously exposed to the environment of authoritarian control, were accustomed to government justified on the basis of force. The idea that government was above self-interested political activity (which only served to subvert the public's welfare) was communicated by colonial administrators. As a result, the notion that authoritarianism was an appropriate mode of rule was to shape the political landscape of the continent for over three decades after independence.

The political legacies of authoritarian rule under colonialism and its implications for post-colonial leadership are at best only a partial explanation for the weakness of political legitimacy in Africa. Certainly, it must not serve to detract attention from the obvious failings of the political elite. State effectiveness has continually waned as a result of the ongoing parochialization of the public realm. Resources allocation by government and other state institutions has typically come to follow ethnic or religious lines. This use of power by the political elite has been very detrimental to the sociopolitical and -economic evolution of the continent, not least because it has created a skewed distribution of resources in favour of those groups that have power and wealth. The segmentation of society that has followed has impeded the many reforms of the political structures that possibly could have enhanced Africa's ability to develop sustainably.

The parochialization of the political realm has not only exacerbated the socio-political and -economic disparities between and within African states, but crucially it has also played a central role in institutionalizing corruption (see box 1.1). Owing to an absence of effective structures with

---

Box 1.1 Cures for corruption in Africa

Corruption is widespread in Africa. The motivation to earn income is strong, exacerbated by poverty and by low and declining civil service salaries. Opportunities to engage in corruption are numerous. Monopoly rents can be very large in highly regulated economies. In transition economies, economic rents are particularly large because of the amount of formerly state-owned property that is essentially up for grabs. The discretion of many public officials is also broad in developing and transition countries, and this systematic weakness is exacerbated by poorly defined, ever-changing and poorly disseminated rules and regulations.

Accountability is typically weak. Political competition and civil liberties are often restricted. Laws and principles of ethics in government are poorly developed, if they exist at all, and the legal institutions charged with enforcing them are ill-prepared for this complex job. The watchdog institutions that provide information on which detection and enforcement are based – such as investigators, accountants and the press – are also weak.

There have been some successes in addressing corruption. Broader economic and institutional reforms that have taken place simultaneously, such as those instituted in Uganda in the late 1980s, have had results. Its strategy encompassed economic reforms and deregulation, civil service reform, a strengthened auditor general's office, the appointment of a reputable inspector general empowered to investigate and prosecute corruption, and implementation of a public information campaign against corruption. Botswana is an example of a country with sound economic and public sector management policies that, once instituted, led to honest governance early on; its success has not been principally derived from the more recent advent of its anti-corruption department.

Addressing corruption effectively therefore means addressing its underlying economic, political and institutional causes. The major emphasis must be put on prevention – that is, on reforming economic policies, institutions and incentives. Major economic policy changes that will unambiguously reduce opportunities for corruption include: lowering tariffs and other barriers to international trade; unifying market-determined exchange rates and interest rates; eliminating enterprise subsidies; minimizing regulations, licensing requirements and other barriers to entry for new firms and investors; demonopolizing and privatizing government assets; and providing transparently prudential banking regulations and auditing and accounting standards. The reform of government institutions may include: civil service reform; improved budgeting, financial management and tax administration; and strengthened legal and judicial systems. Such reforms should involve changing government structures and procedures, placing greater focus on internal competition and incentives to complement these broader reforms. The careful and transparent implementation of enforcement measures, such as the prosecuting of prominent corrupt figures, can also have an impact.

A comprehensive list of all possible anti-corruption measures might include many not mentioned above. Emphasis should be placed on selecting the key measures to be implemented, in line with a country's implementation capabilities, during the first and subsequent stages of an anti-corruption campaign. The entrenched nature of systemic corruption requires boldness – incrementalism is unlikely to work.

Continued

In parts of Africa, efforts are being made to confront this problem. The African Union 2003 Convention on Preventing and Combating Corruption contains an action agenda for corruption eradication, and countries that sign up to it are required to conform to the tenets of the convention. In much of southern Africa, efforts are targeted at four levels – prevention, investigation, prosecution and civic awareness. Several improvements have also been observed in some countries since the Lima Declaration – which highlighted the need for a global coalition targeted at the institution of transparency, accountability and integrity.

autonomy and strength to check corruption, the governing elites of most African states have engaged in high and sometimes egregious levels of corruption, increasingly diverting states' resources for personal gains. In countries such as Nigeria, Sierra Leone, the Democratic Republic of the Congo, the Central African Republic and Zimbabwe, corruption is so extensive that it is viewed as a way of life. Making or receiving bribes is considered a practical method for supplementing one's interest and achieving economic security far in excess of individual ability. An unpublished report from the UN into corruption in fifteen African countries suggests that nearly 30 per cent of annual government budgets is misappropriated by corrupt governing elites. Corruption has also served to fuel the continent's political instability. Between 1970 and 2003, more than thirty-five wars were fought in Africa, with the vast majority of them intra-state in origin – reflecting the power struggle between dominant elites for wealth and influence.

The Context of Socio-economic Decline

We . . . have failed in Africa, along with everybody else. We have not fully understood the problems. We have not identified the priorities. We have not always designed our projects to fit. . . . But we will continue to try. (Written response to a series of questions submitted by the author to James Wolfensohn)

This admission of 'failure' was made by James Wolfensohn while he was still in office, a rarity for a presiding president of the most powerful lending institution in the world – the World Bank. It is, however, a sober realization of the challenges posed to policy makers and the international community as they seek to reverse the continent's socio-economic and -political decline.

In the period immediately after independence there was a net positive inflow of foreign investment and assistance and population growth was lower than it is today; as a result, African economies performed relatively well in aggregate terms from 1960 to the early 1970s. During this period, gross domestic product (GDP) and exports grew at rates comparable to those in the other main developing regions and more rapidly in general than those in South Asia (see table 1.1). Most notably, manufacturing production rose at sustained rates, although from very low levels and in sectors such as food processing, textiles, construction material and other simple consumer goods, which employed relatively unsophisticated technologies. This production effort was accompanied by massive expansion in primary education and significant mobilization of domestic savings that raised the investment ratios from 14 per cent in 1963 to 20 per cent in 1980. Similar progress was achieved in adult literacy and to a lesser extent in health care.

Today, the picture could not be more different. The latest economic indicators from the African Development Report 2005 underline the extent of Africa's socio-economic condition. The Report's celebrated headline growth of 3.5 per cent in GDP in 2004 compared to 3.2 per cent in 2003 belies the systematic decline observable in real per capita GDP growth from 1.0 per cent to 0.8 per cent in the same period. In developmental terms, this means that the combined

Table 1.1 Selected macro-economic indicators, sub-Saharan Africa and South Asia, 1963–80

	GDP		Agriculture		Manufacturing		Export	
	1963–73	1973–80	1963–73	1973–80	1963–73	1973–80	1963–73	1973–80
Sub-Saharan								
Africa	6.0	2.8	2.2	0.0	10.7	10.2	16.9	–0.6
South Asia	3.7	4.3	3.4	2.4	4.1	5.2	–0.7	5.8

Sources: UNECA, 2000; World Bank, 1981, 1999

economies of Africa actually shrunk by 0.2 per cent in the twelve months up to the end of 2004. To put this in context, all other regions in the world are already outperforming Africa, and efforts to redress this poor performance over the past two decades have not been successful. In 2003, for example, the average gross national product (GNP) per capita in the Organization for Economic Co-operation and Development (OECD) countries was $28,086, compared with $528 in Africa. This means that the industrialized countries are roughly fifty-one times wealthier than African states. Assuming that the OECD countries could stop stretching this development gap further, and hoping that African economies could grow at an annual rate of 3.5 per cent over the coming years, it would take the continent some 135 years to reach today's level of wealth enjoyed by OECD countries.

According to recent United Nations data, in 2004 some 80 per cent of the low human development countries – these are countries with high population growth rates, low income, low literacy and low life expectancy – were located in Africa (UNDP 2002). There are only ten African countries in the middle category – Algeria, Botswana, Egypt, Gabon, Libya, Mauritius, Morocco, Seychelles, Swaziland and South Africa; five of these have a combined population of just 4.6 million – Mauritius, Seychelles, Botswana, Gabon and Swaziland. The remaining forty-two countries on the continent are in the low human development category.

This, however, does not tell the entire story. There are fifty-five countries in this category, which means that African countries account for 76 per cent of the category. Even more telling is that, of the thirty countries with the lowest human development indices, twenty-six (or 87 per cent) are African. Not surprisingly, poverty has increased at a faster rate on the continent than anywhere else in the world. With a fifth of the world population, the continent is home to one in three poor persons in the world, and four of every ten of its inhabitants live in what the World Bank (1999) classifies as 'a condition of absolute poverty' (p. 10). More worrying still, Africa is the only region in the world where both the absolute number and the proportion of poor people are expected to increase during this millennium (UNDP, 2000).

Nearly half the population of Africa (300 million people) live on less than $1 a day: if current trends continue, by 2015 Africa will account for 50 per cent of the poor of the developing world (up from 25 per cent in 1990). During the 1990s the region experienced a decline in GDP per capita of 0.6 per cent per annum, and because economic growth was highly skewed between countries, approximately half the total population were actually poorer in 2004 than they were in 1990. Income and wealth distributions are also extremely unequal in many countries, and with improved growth rates such inequalities are likely to increase rather than to diminish (World Bank, 2003b). Table 1.2 and table 1.3 provide a summary of both income and non-income poverty indicators for Africa and an indication of how this poverty picture has changed over the recent past. The data are sourced from the Chronic Poverty Report (2004) and the World Bank's World Development Indicators (WDIs). These poverty figures enable international and inter-regional poverty comparisons to be drawn.

Understanding the Stagnation and Decline

So, what went wrong? There is no single explanation for Africa's rapid and sustained economic retrogression. Instead, there is a confluence of factors ranging from poor policies at both macro and micro levels to declining terms of trade, famine and the corrosive effects of political instability on economic systems over time.

Poor Policies

At independence, rapid industrialization was believed to be the key to an equally rapid economic growth. Agriculture, rather than being supported, was taxed heavily to provide

Table 1.2 Summary of poverty indicators for Africa

Region	Population	Population below $1 day (%) (1989–99)	Population below $2 day (%) (1993–2000)	Infant mortality rate per 1,000 live births per year (2000)	Under-5 mortality rate (per 1,000 live births 2001)	Life expectancy years (2000)		Adult illiteracy rate (%) (2000)	
						M	F	M	F
West Africa	260,142,000	58	76	111	185	50	51	35	52
Central Africa	72,950,000	50	87	121	196	47	50	28	49
Southern Africa	113,039,000	29	62	111	165	45	47	19	29
East Africa	181,051,140	30	79	100	155	47	49	31	47
Sub-Saharan Africa	628,182,140	43	76	109	174	48	50	30	46
North Africa	169,053,500	3	21	44	53	64	68	30	53

Figures have been rounded
Sources: Chronic Poverty Research Centre, 2004; World Bank 2003b

Table 1.3 African poverty, 1980–2003

Region	Change in infant mortality rate (%)	Change in life expectancy (years)		Change in adult illiteracy (%)		Average annual change in household consumption per capita (%)
		M	F	M	F	
West Africa	-18	2	1	-25	-29	-3.9
Central Africa	-5	-2	-5	-23	-28	-0.8
Southern Africa	-6	-6	-8	-13	-15	-0.3
East Africa	-17	-1	-3	-18	-25	-0.3
Sub-Saharan Africa	-15	-1	-3	-21	-25	-2.3
North Africa	-56	10	11	-19	-24	1.2

Figures have been rounded

West Africa = Benin, Burkina Faso, Cameroon, Cape Verde, Chad, Côte d'Ivoire, Equatorial Guinea, Gabon, the Gambia, Ghana, Guinea, Guinea-Bissau, Liberia, Mali, Mauritania, Niger, Nigeria, São Tomé, Senegal, Sierra Leone, Togo

Central Africa = Burundi, Central African Republic, Democratic Republic of Congo, Rwanda

Southern Africa = Angola, Botswana, Lesotho, Malawi, Mozambique, Namibia, South Africa, Swaziland, Zambia, Zimbabwe

East Africa = Comoros, Djibouti, Eritrea, Ethiopia, Kenya, Madagascar, Mauritius, Somalia, Tanzania, Uganda

North Africa = Algeria, Egypt, Libya, Morocco, Sudan, Tunisia

Source: Chronic Poverty Research Centre, 2004; World Bank, 2003b

resources for the industrial sector. Across the continent, governments drew up five-year plans, created public enterprises and enacted regulations to control prices, restrict trade and allocate foreign earnings in pursuit of social goals. At the same time, countries were struggling to establish themselves as nations and put effective governmental structures in place. But governments became over-extended, particularly relative to their weak institutional base, as they tried to build national unity and deliver on the promise of independence.

Exogenous Shocks

In the 1970s a number of factors outside the continent served to expose the weaknesses of the prevailing development strategies. It began when in 1973 the Organization of Petroleum-Exporting Countries (OPEC) agreed to a dramatic increase in oil prices, which immediately affected the supply of foreign exchange of African countries. The price increase benefited a few of Africa's oil-producing countries (Nigeria, Gabon, Angola and Congo) by increasing their supply of foreign exchange. However, it was an economic disaster for most African countries and severely depleted their reserves of foreign exchange while simultaneously increasing their already heavy burden of debt as they attempted to continue to maintain imports of petroleum necessary for continuing their economic development plans.

Natural Disasters

The impact of the oil crisis was compounded by a severe drought that stretched across the continent in 1972–3. Hundred of thousands of refugees fled the drought-stricken areas, flocking to the cities or seeking new pastures, often crossing borders into other countries. Agricultural production decreased dramatically, and livestock starved to death. The affected countries required immediate supplies of imported food and food aid to prevent mass starvation of their population. This put a further burden on foreign exchange reserves and increased the debt of many countries. These mainly external factors in combination with domestic policy shortcomings resulted in a slowing of economic growth. A similar oil crisis in 1978 and declining world prices for the primary commodity exports of Africa, along with continued domestic policy deficiencies, led to a period of actual economic decline in the 1980s.

Commodity Price Decline

Over the same period, the price of most of Africa's raw material exports declined in relation to imported machinery, spare parts, other finished goods and oil. Thus, between 1967/8 and 1986/7, Africa's share in global primary product export declined by half, from 8.3 per cent to 4.2 per cent (UNCTAD, 1999, p. 24). During the 1980s, short periods of price recovery were superimposed upon a relentless downward trend. The volume of world trade, which had expanded at 5.7 per cent yearly in the 1970s, virtually stagnated between 1981 and 1983. With average annual GNP growth rate of Africa's trading partners falling from 4.4 per cent in the 1970s to 1.8 per cent between 1980 and 1983, the growth rates of the demand for primary products and for fuel dropped between the 1970s and 1981–3 from 2.0 and 0.5 per cent to 1.0 and −11.0 per cent per year, respectively (IMF, 1989). While African exports stagnated completely and thus lost market share, the overall decline in world demand and in the price for primary commodities would have led in any case to a serious decline in Africa's export earnings.

By 1993, real non-oil commodity prices had fallen to less than half their 1988 levels (World Bank, 1993). In the case of tropical beverages such as coffee and cocoa, the decline was even more severe than the average, with prices falling by almost 70 per cent (World Bank, 1993, p. 7). Translated into financial terms, the cumulative losses suffered by devel-

Table 1.4 Average annual growth in per capita GDP in regions and countries of the world, 1960–98

	1960–9	1970–9	1980–91	1990–8
Sub-Saharan Africa	1.2	1.6	−0.6	0.6
Developing				
countries	1.9	2.3	0.0	1.3
Latin America	2.2	2.3	−0.8	1.0
OECD countries	4.2	2.6	1.6	2.7
World	2.4	2.4	0.3	1.6

Source: World Bank and IMF, various reports

oping countries amounted to over $290 bn between 1980 and 1991 (Maizels, 1995). For sub-Saharan Africa, the most seriously affected region, the loss was equivalent to 6 per cent of GDP.

Declining Terms of Trade

With the sharp downturn in commodity prices and the increase in the prices of manufacturing products, the overall terms of trade of Africa fell by 7 per cent between 1981 and 1985 (IMF, 1989). Nominal interest rates on the foreign debt mushroomed to record high levels of 18–20 per cent during 1980–3. The decline in nominal rates observed since then has not been paralleled by a commensurate decline in real interest rates. Gross capital flows declined sharply after 1983. Net capital flows dropped even more dramatically, from $10 billion in 1982 to about $2.5 billion in 1985. The resulting government indebtedness and lack of economic growth reduced Africa's significance as an export market. Poor economic performance, combined with political instability and deteriorating infrastructure, discouraged new private investment and lending, and even precipitated some disinvestment (Callaghy, 1991, p. 41).

Table 1.5 Foreign direct investment (as percentage of global FDI flows), 1997–2002

Indicators	1997	1998	1999	2000	2001	2002
Developed countries	56.8	69.8	77.2	79.1	80.1	
Developing countries and economies	39.2	27.2	20.7	18.9	18.0	
Asia	22.4	13.8	9.3	11.3	11.2	
Latin America	14.9	12.0	10.3	6.8	6.8	
Africa	2.3	1.2	1.0	0.7	0.7	
Africa (as a percentage of developing countries)	5.88	4.63	4.72	3.78	3.87	3.11

Sources: ADB, 2003; IMF, 2003; UNCTAD, 2002; UNDP, 2002

Why Africa Had to Adjust

In the early 1980s, symptoms of the malaise were evident almost everywhere on the continent. The returns on investment by the World Bank were much lower in Africa than in other regions. It was – and still is – impossible to attract foreign private capital, either in investment or in loans, and portfolio investment flows were negligible (see table 1.5). The international price for Africa's government debt in secondary markets was the lowest for developing countries, reflecting the markets' perception of the continent as uncreditworthy. The physical infrastructure, already poor, deteriorated from lack of maintenance, and the quality of government services declined, fuelling among other things civil discontent and corruption.

In pursuit of appropriate mitigation strategies, the World Bank and the IMF identified domestic policy weakness of African states as the main culprit in accounting for the continent's dire economic position. Based on this assumption, African governments were 'encouraged' to adopt SAPs as a crucial prerequisite to receiving vitally needed loans. The word 'encouraged' is used very loosely here, because in almost all cases there was little choice on the part of the recipient states but to follow the recommendations from the IMF and the World Bank.

The goals of SAPs were to alter the domestic policies of African governments by shifting the emphasis from state-led development to market-driven approaches with a particular emphasis on sound fiscal and macro-economic prudence. This required a tightening of fiscal and credit policies to correct the decades of fiscal imbalances resulting from high government spending. Budget deficits in excess of 7 per cent of GDP were the norm. While this budget deficit ratio was not much larger than those elsewhere, the ratio of government expenditure as a percentage of GDP was significantly higher. This was in large part to service the needs of the rapid industrialization programmes embarked on after independence.

Two broad policy components came to characterize SAPs: short- to medium-term macro-economic stabilization measures to restore internal and external balances, which fell within the purview of the IMF (see table 1.6); and SAPs proper, which were designed to 'unleash market forces so that competition could help improve the allocation of resources by getting price signals right and creating a climate that allowed business to respond to those signals in ways which could increase the returns to investment' (World Bank, 1994, p. 61) (see table 1.7). In the process, SAPs led to a radical rationalization of the recipient governments' expenditure commitments mainly – but not exclusively – in areas concerned with the provisions of welfare (i.e. health, education and basic sustenance such as food subsidies).

Table 1.6 IMF adjustment policies

Policies – macro-economic adjustment (stabilization)	Economic objectives
Devaluation.	To promote exports and reduce demand for imports by raising their prices.
Public spending reduction on: wages; employment; investment; subsidies; etc. Tax increases: taxes on incomes; taxes on spending.	To reduce the budget deficit and thus: • slow down the growth of government debt; • slow down the growth of the money supply; and • reduce overall demand, and thus demand for imports.
Tighter monetary and credit policies and higher interest rates.	To reduce overall demand, and thus demand for imports; to limit or reduce the rate of inflation.

These measures were meant to help countries resolve balance-of-payments problems, to reduce inflation, and to prevent future economic crisis by promoting longer-term structural reforms. Often they led to periods of economic austerity as government expenditure was slashed and market forces were unleashed. The World Bank euphemistically called this process 'crossing the desert', and argued that short-term pain was necessary for long-term success in economic growth and improvements in the quality of life.

The 'short-term pain' provoked a storm of criticism, especially from African governments and NGOs. They were joined by international agencies such as the United Nations

Table 1.7 World Bank adjustment policies

Policies – structural adjustment	Economic objectives
Reducing the role of the state: restricting government spending; privatization; deregulation of markets.	To increase economic efficiency, and thus improve long-term economic performance.
'Getting the prices right': freeing interest rates; freeing exchange rates; freeing wages; freeing prices; agricultural produce price increases; parastatal price increases; subsidy reductions; tax reforms; cost recovery.	
Opening the economy: trade reform; foreign investment reform.	
Institutional strengthening and capacity-building.	

Children's Fund (UNICEF), which in 1987 made a funda-mental challenge to the adjustment paradigm by publishing *Adjustment with a Human Face* – a multi-country study of the effects of IMF policies on children. In response, both the World Bank and the IMF said they would prioritize the social sectors and poverty reduction concerns in their policies and even admitted that their initial attempts in the early 1980s to push through adjustment whatever the price caused unnecessary hardship. Yet the main policy thrusts of adjustment programmes remain in place today and both

Table 1.8 GDP growth under adjustment – agriculture growth rate (median), sub-Saharan Africa, 1981–6, 1987–91 and 1992–7

	1981–6	1987–91	1992–7
Large improvements	4.2	2.4	2.0
Small improvements	3.1	2.8	2.1
Deterioration	2.3	3.3	2.8
All countries	3.1	2.8	2.2

Sources: ADB, 2003; IMF, 2003

institutions still tend to maintain that where programmes fail it is because of inadequate implementation on the part of national governments.

What Adjustment Achieved

Table 1.8 represents sectoral figures for the impact of SAPs on agricultural growth over a twenty-year period. It is clear from the table that SAPs had very little impact on the sector. The more worrying observation is that the trend can be replicated across all the major indicators of economic growth. In almost all its evaluation reports (World Bank, 1989, 1990, 1994, 1996, 1998), the World Bank observed this trend, but attributed its causes not to the poor designs of SAPs, but to their implementation. In its words, 'no African country has achieved a sound macro-economic policy stance, and there is considerable concern that the reforms undertaken to date are fragile and that they are merely returning the continent to the slow growth path of the 1960s and early 1970s' (World Bank, 1998, p. 14).

In truth, it is not clear whether the lack of effective implementation results from African governments' unwillingness to undertake reforms (as the World Bank claims) or from the objective conditions of the economies not permitting the kind of adjustment being recommended. Despite nearly two and half decades of adjustment policies, this debate remains largely unresolved. The only certainty, however, is that SAPs often have an immediate and at times detrimental impact on the welfare of the poorest members of society, especially as they affect food prices, costs of education and payment of medical services (see table 1.9). Parfitt and Riley (1989) argue that the deprivations experienced by certain groups who 'have been deprived of their stake in society by some aspect of an austerity program that has moved them towards or below the poverty line' result in violence. For example, state employees who have been laid off become more critical of the regime and become actively opposed to the economic policies which they see as disadvantaging them. Thus, Parfitt and Riley argue that the overall result of such economic policies is often 'to destabilize the recipient states as key groups in the populace rebel against the combination of rising prices and declining real wages and public services'.

Lipumba (1994) observes that the dominant 'opinion among African intellectuals is that structural adjustment programs are part of the problem rather than part of the solution' (p. 32). Certainly, SAPs have done little to foster the social, political and economic conditions that could contribute to the development of stable state–society relations in Africa and the creation of a stable social order. The promotion of exports for debt repayment and the cutting of public expenditure on welfare are tantamount to a scandal in a region where 100 million people are undernourished; where there is one doctor for 36,000 people, compared with one for 400 people in industrial countries; and where nine out of ten of the HIV-infected people worldwide reside. One author has even referred to SAPs as a form of economic genocide. 'When compared to genocide in various periods of colonial history, its impact is devastating. Structural adjustment programs directly affect the livelihood of more than 4 billion people' (Chossudovsky, 1994, p. 20).

SAPs raise particular problems for African governments because most of the factors fuel the AIDS pandemic (see

Table 1.9 Impact of common structural adjustment measures on health determinants

Intended result	Policy	Common impact on the poor
Reduced budget deficit, freeing up money for debt servicing	Reducing government expenditure	Reduced health, education and social welfare spending and the introduction of cost-recovery and user fees put health care and education beyond the reach of many ordinary people. Public sector redundancies and salary freezes lead to fewer teachers and doctors.
Increased efficiency	Privatization of state-run industries	Massive lay-offs and increased unemployment with no social security provision push families deeper into poverty.
Increased exports, boosting foreign exchange reserves needed for debt repayment	Currency devaluation and export promotion	Cost of imports soars, including vital resources such as imported medicines. Moreover, export prices fall because many countries are promoting the same exports under SAPs, so countries are still no better off.
Reduced inflation	Raising interest rates	Farmers and small companies can no longer afford to borrow money and are forced to reduce production or go out of business.
Increased efficiency in food production	Removal of price controls	Basic food prices rise, putting even further pressure on already stretched household budgets.

table 1.10). The health of the poor is a particular case in point. A primary aim of adjustment policies has been to give more incentive to production in the rural economy. In sub-Saharan Africa, in particular, most poverty is located in the countryside; raising the world market prices for tradeable agricultural goods by reducing export taxes and devaluing the currency would, it was argued, increase rural incomes. The reality, however, has been different: rural producers have not been able to expand production of tradeable goods (or switch production from one crop to another) because they lack the necessary infrastructure (roads and storage buildings, for example) to bring their produce to market. In this respect adjustment policies have had the opposite effect because cuts in government expenditure are often the main reason why infrastructure is dilapidated. Moreover, a shift by rural producers away from food ('untradeable') to non-food ('tradeable') in response to policy stimulus has contributed to the decline in food production in sub-Saharan Africa, which is lower today than it was in 1980, with potentially serious consequences for nutritional outcomes.

At a time when up to 70 per cent of adults in some hospitals are suffering from AIDS-related illnesses – placing extreme pressure on health services – many African countries are still cutting health expenditure in order to satisfy IMF and World Bank conditionalities. For example, in Tanzania – where over half a million children are orphans as a result of AIDS (UNAIDS, 2002) – the government spends only around $3.20 per person per year on health provision, a quarter of what the World Bank itself estimates is necessary to provide basic care (World Bank, 2002). The Tanzanian government spends in excess of three times more on debt servicing each year than it does on health care. Similarly, in Malawi, where nearly 16 per cent of the population are living with either HIV or AIDS, and where there is only one doctor for every 50,000 people, government spending on health care was dwarfed by debt repayment by two to one – (see table 1.11).

The consequences of the continuing low levels of health expenditure in poor countries are apparent in a country such

Table 1.10 Circle of decline and vulnerability: the impacts of SAPs on African societies

Policy	Policy response	Domestic impact	Implications for the spread of HIV/AIDS
To reduce government expenditure	Introduce user fee for health services	Reduced access to health services; decline in general health of the population	Reduced awareness of health issues, including HIV/AIDS; poor general health; reduced treatment for opportunistic infections – particularly STDs
	Introduce user fee for education	Children, particularly girls, removed from schools; marginalization of large section of population to informal sectors like prostitution, with associated risk	Reduced education; increased illiteracy; increased risk of HIV transmission due to poor educational knowledge; particular vulnerability of women due to lack of formal education
	Decrease spending on health and education	Reduced quality and quantity of facilities; lack of equipment; fewer and less trained staff	Increased vulnerability to infection

	Public sector redundancies and wage freezes	Unemployment; staff shortages leading to reduced quality and quantity of education and health services	Increased vulnerability to infection
	Removal of price subsidies on food, fuel and other basic commodities	Reduced quality and quantity of food; declining calorie consumption per head	Poor health means greater vulnerability to infection, increase in informal sector activities with greater risk of HIV infection
	Reduced civil services	Reduced administrative capacity	Governments less able to promote AIDS prevention
To increase export earnings	Promote large export-orientated projects	Workers migrate to jobs from home; decrease in food production; restructuring of domestic production patterns leading to decrease in consumable food for domestic societies; rural-to-urban migration	Workers more likely to engage in risky behaviour with increased risk of HIV/AIDS contraction; spreading of HIV through migration; returning migrants infecting local communities

Table 1.11 Debt to health and education profile, selected African countries

Country	Percentage of population with HIV/AIDS[a]	Percentage of govt. spending on primary education[b]	Percentage of govt. spending on health[c]	Percentage of govt. spending on debt servicing (2004)[d]
Malawi	15.5	15.8	14.5	34
Mozambique	13.0	20.2	11.1	57
Rwanda	8.9	9.2	9.8	32
Tanzania	7.8	25.4	14.9	42
Uganda	5.9	21.1	9.3	39
Zambia	21.5	14.6	12.6	62

Sources: [a]UNAIDS, 2004; [b]World Bank, 2004; [c]WHO/UNAIDS/International AIDS Society, 2004; [d]UNDP, 2004

as Zambia (see below). Some of the worst effects come through the implementation of user fees. In the face of declining expenditure on public services, many countries have introduced user charges as a way to finance the health care system and discourage unnecessary use. However, their effect has been quite damaging. Evidence from several countries shows that they rarely raise significant levels of revenue for the health sector and have regressive effects in terms of equity. Studies from Nigeria, Zimbabwe and Algeria show that when user charges were implemented for maternity services, the use of antenatal care declined and maternal mortality and emergency deliveries in hospitals increased. When the World Bank advised Kenya to introduce a user fee of $2.15 for its STD clinics, attendance fell by between 35 and 60 per cent, a particularly worrying result as STD treatment is important to HIV prevention.

Meeting the Millennium Development Goals (MDGs)

It follows that to achieve the MDG of a 50 per cent reduction by 2015 in the proportion of people in Africa whose incomes are less than $1 a day, very rapid GDP growth will be required if the poorest are to benefit. This is currently not happening on key indicators, the prevailing evidence indicating that the situation on the ground is getting worse. Take the following key areas: eradicating extreme poverty and hunger; achieving universal primary education; improving maternal health and child mortality.

Eradicating Extreme Poverty and Hunger

Many African countries made very little progress in eradicating hunger and malnutrition in the 1990s. It is estimated that the number of people suffering malnutrition has increased to some 200 million in recent decades and the problem is especially severe in central, eastern and southern Africa, where almost a half of the population of 360 million is estimated as being undernourished. Women and children are especially vulnerable to food insecurity and malnutrition, with the latter being especially important as a cause of under-5 mortality. Trends were actually reversed during the 1990s in those countries most affected by adverse growth in GDP and by the effects of HIV/AIDS. Indeed UNDP/UNICEF recently concluded that, 'During the 1990s, the spread of HIV/AIDS had a devastating effect on families and communities. The loss of productive capacity among families affected by HIV/AIDS had a major impact on food production and on nutritional well-being' (UNDP, 2004, p. 54).

Achieving Universal Primary Education

The target is that by 2015 children everywhere, boys and girls, will be able to complete a full course of primary schooling. While African countries saw some progress in educating children during the 1990s, this was not nearly enough to meet the goal set for 2015. In over a third of countries every other child is not in school; while some countries have increased their enrolment rates (such as Uganda and Malawi), other countries actually experienced declines (such as the Central African Republic, Lesotho and South Africa). There continue to be significant urban–rural gaps in enrolment, and in some countries the enrolment ratio in urban areas is some two to three times higher than for rural populations. Unless the educational targets are substantially achieved in the coming decade, then not only will millions of children be deprived of their right to basic education but many of the other targets will also be unachievable. A better-educated population is essential for the achievement of democratic states in Africa and for improvement in systems of governance. It is wholly improbable that economic growth and poverty reduction targets can be met without a better-educated and skilled population, and a more educated population is essential for improving labour productivity. Improved access to education for girls is also crucial for achieving progress on maternal and under-5 mortality rates, and for progress generally in the area of reproductive health – see below.

Improving Maternal Health and Reducing Child Mortality

This MDG encompasses two aims: to reduce by two-thirds the under-5 mortality rate by 2015, and to reduce by three-quarters the maternal mortality ratio by the same date. At the present time 15 per cent of all children in Africa will not live to see their fifth birthday. Progress in reaching the under-5 mortality rate seems to have been reversed during the past two decades, and some countries, such as Botswana and Kenya, have actually seen increases in this rate due to HIV/AIDS. There also remain significant gaps between urban and rural rates in many countries, and it is clear that the probability of a child dying is much greater in poorer families than in richer ones (the probability is twice as high for children in the bottom 20 per cent of the income distribution as it is in the top 20 per cent).

African countries currently account for about one-third of all maternal deaths worldwide, with about 250,000 women dying during pregnancy and childbirth every year. These trends seem if anything to have worsened during the past decade, in part because of deteriorating health care systems. But the primary problem, apart from poor access to health care, continues to be the continued high levels of fertility, and thus persistently high risks of maternal mortality. The comparative rates of maternal mortality between developing regions strikingly emphasize the gap between Africa and other regions – in Africa a woman faces a 1 in 13 chance of dying in childbirth compared with 1 in 160 in Latin America and 1 in 280 in East Asia.

Debt, HIPC and the Struggle against HIV/AIDS

In aggregate terms, the total long-term debt of Africa stood at $340 billion in 2002. Although this figure is quite modest by global standards – Brazil, for example, owed more than $120 billion at the end of 2000 – compared to the continent's ability to repay, this debt is enormous. Africans can only pay off the debt with earnings in foreign currency. That is, they must use money from exports, from aid, or from new foreign loans. Take the case of Ethiopia. Its debt of $10 billion ($179 a person) at the end of 2000 may not seem like much compared to the $11 billion Europe spent on ice cream in 1997. But it was almost thirteen times the amount the country earned in exports in 1999. Ethiopia used the equivalent of 45 per cent of its $783 million in export earnings on debt payments. Even after such a crushing payout, Ethiopia's debt is still unbearable. Or consider the trade-offs with investments in health care. In 2004, 70 per cent of the world's new AIDS infections were in sub-Saharan Africa. So were four-fifths of all deaths from AIDS that year. Yet among all African countries only South Africa is spending more on health care than on debt service. For most African countries, the entire annual health budget is less than $10 a person. Health care, moreover, is only one of the urgent needs requiring investment. Development aid, which has been in steep decline in recent years, does not make up the gap. In 1996, sub-Saharan African countries were paying out $1.30 on debt service for every $1 received in grant aid from donors.

Against this background, the introduction of the Heavily Indebted Poor Countries (HIPC) initiative in 1996 by the World Bank and IMF appeared as a step in the right direction, not least because it seemed to recognize the impossibility of resolving the continent's debt crisis just by postponing payments (the now infamous rescheduling policies of the late 1980s and early 1990s). Some debt, creditors acknowledged, would have to be cancelled, including debt owed to the multilateral institutions themselves (almost one-third of Africa's debt). Creditors agreed that, in principle, as much as 80 per cent of external debt could be cancelled. The unanswered questions, however, were under what conditions, how much, how fast and who would pay for it (Cheru, 2002). Typically, the international financial institutions imposed rigid economic adjustment programmes as a condition for participation in HIPC. By September 1998, only eight countries, including five in Africa, had qualified for debt relief packages adding up to about $6.5 billion. Uganda was the only African country that had actually reached the 'completion point', receiving about $650 million in debt reduction (WHO, 2004). To supplement World Bank and IMF funds, fifteen donor countries (not including the US) had paid or pledged about $300 million for the initiative by late 1998.

In 2000, the HIPC II initiative proposed incremental, but noteworthy, steps towards the modernization of the original HIPC initiative. Chief among these were the proposal to grant larger reductions of the total accumulated debt (the debt overhang), quicker reductions in debt service payments, and finally placing poverty reduction at the heart of an enhanced new framework. The devil, however, was in the detail. The eligibility for debt relief under the Enhanced HIPC Initiative was conditional upon 'good performance' in the implementation of an enhanced structural adjustment programme (which was supposed to become the Poverty Reduction and Growth Facility – PRGF) for a period of three years instead of six years under the original HIPC. Having reached the decision point after the first three years of good economic performance, the country must then demonstrate that its debt servicing is unsustainable, following designated threshold values with respect to the ratio of debt to exports, and the ratio of debt to fiscal revenues.[1] If the country finally qualifies for relief, its debt servicing is brought down to what is deemed within the terms of the initiative to be a sustainable level only after reaching the completion point, or a further three-year waiting period.

This less than generous arrangement still left countries diverting a sizeable portion of their scarce foreign exchange earnings towards debt servicing for an indefinite period of time. Moreover, while expenditures on education and health services will be expanded under the new HIPC II, the structural factors that induced poverty were not addressed by conventional structural adjustment programmes.[2] More worryingly, while debt relief is important in the short run, the extent to which additional fresh resources will be available for HIPC countries is not certain. Debt relief alone is not going to be enough to put these broken countries on a path of sustained growth.

There exists a great deal of scepticism about the willingness of Western creditor countries, the multilateral development banks in particular, to break the chain of debt bondage of the HIPC countries, not to mention the adequacy of funding for HIPC to wipe the slate clean. Conditionality and external control remain the core guiding principles of the Enhanced HIPC Initiative, despite the claims of the architect of the plan that poverty eradication is the real objective of the Initiative (Hansen-Kuhn and Hellinger, 1999). Moreover, linking debt relief to successful implementation of 'good governance' is a major mistake and this is bound to delay much-needed relief to countries desperately in need of fresh resources to fix broken-down social systems (EURODAD, 1999). Past experience shows that many African governments have failed to meet such conditionalities of adjustment and reform. In fact, in recent years, three out of four Enhanced Structural Adjustment Facility (ESAF) programmes have broken down because their conditions were too tough to be fulfilled.

Take the case of Zambia: its debt servicing has, on average, been absorbing nearly a third of the country's export earnings. In 2001 Zambia paid $125 million in debt service payment to Paris Club creditors and the multilateral institutions. This amount represented a significant portion of overall government expenditure, equal to 69 per cent of the amount budgeted for all social sectors combined that same year. As a result, the ability of public sector institutions effectively to implement HIV/AIDS prevention and control activities has been significantly hampered.

The government of Zambia, working with several local NGOs and church organizations, has proposed a multi-donor debt relief programme to accelerate the national response to

HIV/AIDS. Under this proposal, scarce national funds which now go to service the debt would be set aside for investment in activities that will control the spread of HIV/AIDS. The funds would then be used by both civil sector groups and public social sector institutions to implement activities nationwide, which would be designed to prevent HIV/AIDS, manage existing cases and address the growing orphans crisis. The combined civil and public sector response would be part of the overall National HIV/AIDS Strategy developed by the multi-sectoral HIV/AIDS Council and Secretariat. The estimated amount required for channelling into HIV/AIDS prevention and impact mitigation programmes, as a result of debt relief, is $89 million over a five-year period.[3] This averages to be nearly $18 million per year to cover all programmes in both public sector and civil society. An independent non-government body will manage the fund, and it will be governed by a Debt Relief Steering Committee composed of representatives from the NGOs, government and the donor community. This will ensure financial and programmatic accountability.

Like that of many of the countries on the continent, Zambia's progress towards qualification for debt relief under the Enhanced HIPC Initiative hinges largely on the government's capacity to show real and tangible progress on the promise it made during the last consultative group meeting to institute fundamental governance reform. While there is little wrong with this in principle, the fear is that the critical resources needed to tackle the AIDS epidemic might be held up indefinitely if progress on governance reform falters. As a consequence, the excellent work that the NGOs and civil society are doing to prevent the spread of HIV/AIDS with meagre resources will be completely wiped out. In the context of the epidemic, action is needed now, and not three years down the road, by which time millions more Africans will have been infected or died of the HIV virus. That would be a great humanitarian tragedy for which the international community would ultimately be held responsible.

Concluding Remarks

Poverty, marginalization and widespread alienation remain the most significant and pervasive problems facing African countries. These are also the root drivers for the continent's HIV/AIDS epidemic. As succeeding chapters will illustrate, this confluence of factors not only increases the risk of vulnerable individuals and groups contracting the HIV virus, it also serves to impede their ability to respond to the multiple demands of the disease. The result is greater vulnerability to HIV/AIDS.

These problems cannot be adequately addressed until the current approach to macro-economic adjustment and rules governing international trade is fundamentally altered. The Copenhagen Declaration on Social Development (para. 91), for example, called on governments to ensure that social development goals are included in SAPS and that basic social programmes and expenditures are protected from budget reduction. The impact of SAPS should be reviewed and altered to reduce their negative effects and improve their positive impacts. The emphasis of such programmes should no longer be on how to achieve economic growth, but rather on what kind of growth is being achieved, by whom, and to what end. At the same time, political and social leaders on the continent should shoulder a huge responsibility for dragging their societies out of the deprivation they are in – after all, they are hugely culpable.

2
Understanding the Dynamics of HIV/AIDS in Africa

Introduction

Across the African continent, HIV/AIDS is savagely cutting life expectancy, which is now about twenty years less than it would have been without the epidemic, and below forty years in some countries. Like all events on such a scale, the impact of HIV/AIDS on the continent ranges far beyond the harrowing catalogue of lives lost, into the prosperity or poverty of nations, the character of government and the fabric of social and community life. In this sense, the epidemic could be seen as a survival issue for the continent. Not only does it spell an early and painful death for millions of individuals, it also threatens to derail the continent's prospects for development and governance. Owing to HIV/AIDS, many countries across Africa are now witnessing deterioration in child survival rates, reduced life expectancy, crumbling and/or over-burdened health systems and fragmenting socio-cultural coping networks. In both men and women, the epidemic is disproportionately affecting the most productive members of African societies – prime-aged adults – robbing these societies of scarce skills, children of their parents and a continent of a generation in the prime of their active lives. As a result, HIV/AIDS is distorting the very

fabric of everyday life on the continent, with profound implications for social cohesion, economic development and, ultimately, political stability.

In order to understand the scale of Africa's HIV/AIDS-led
crisis, one must proceed from the fact that it is complex,
multi-faceted and influenced by many medical, social, economic and cultural factors. As remarked in chapter 1, the
evidence is quite mixed with respect to the extent to which
different factors contribute to the spread and entrenchment
of the epidemic across the continent, but it is only after
understanding the complexity of these factors that we can
begin to improve the efficacy of policy response. This chapter
aims to provide a state-of-the-art analysis of some of the
dominant drivers of the HIV/AIDS epidemic in Africa. In
the process, it will argue that sexual behaviour and patterns
are only one set of many factors working to expose Africans
disproportionately to the risk of contracting HIV. The
chapter begins with a brief discussion of the origins of HIV,
and then moves to analyse the patterns of prevalence in
Africa. It concludes by assessing the complex array of factors
known to be fanning the HIV/AIDS epidemic on the
continent.

On the Origins of HIV

The Human Immunodeficiency Virus (HIV) is a retrovirus
transmitted primarily through sexual intercourse, but also
through infected blood and from mother to newborn child.
It survives by replicating (reproducing) inside CD4 blood
cells – the very cells which normally protect the body against
infection (see box 2.1). In the first few weeks after entering
the body, HIV spreads rapidly and may cause flu-like symptoms and/or a rash, both of which disappear after a few days.
Then the viral load – the amount of virus in the blood – falls
and for several years most people have no symptoms. During
this time, however, viral load slowly rises again and the
number of CD4 cells falls, making the individual increasingly

---

Box 2.1 Epidemiology: transmission routes

- Sexual transmission – men who have sex with men are most at risk in North America and Western Europe. In developing countries, heterosexual spread constitutes the most important route of transmission.
- Blood/blood products – the sharing of needles by injecting drug users has represented an important route of transmission in Western Europe and North America, and also accounts for an increasing number of HIV transmissions in Eastern Europe and Asia. Haemophiliacs were one of the first risk groups to be identified; they were infected through contaminated blood.
- Vertical transmission – the transmission rate from mother to her child varies from around 2–5 per cent in Western Europe to up to 50 per cent in Africa. Vertical transmission may occur transplacentally, perinatally during the birth process, or postnatally through breast milk.

---

susceptible to 'opportunistic infections' such as tuberculosis that people without HIV are more likely to resist. As the immune system of the HIV positive person slowly weakens, the person progresses towards AIDS. An HIV-infected person is said to have AIDS when a number of factors are present simultaneously. The definitions vary, but generally include the appearance of one or more opportunistic infections together with HIV infection. 'Advanced HIV infection' is sometimes used to refer to a severely weakened immune system irrespective of the presence of other infections.

It is fair to say that for much of the past two or more decades, the rational pursuit of knowledge in the hope of advancing mitigation strategies against the impacts of HIV/AIDS has run parallel to (or often been superseded by) a darker murder-mystery-style motivation of finding a culprit to blame. To some extent, this desire to apportion blame is part of an emotive quest to seek and destroy the villain(s) responsible for the AIDS epidemic, since the wish to hold someone or something accountable for one's misfortune remains a fairly constant human trait. Accordingly, it is possible, as the epidemic enters its third decade, to draw up a list of prime suspects in the hunt for the person or groups of people who brought this misfortune on humankind. The most widely propagated theories on the origins of HIV/AIDS fall into three categories: the religious – talk of God's revenge and divine retribution for sins against moral order; the conspiratorial – that AIDS was the result of biological warfare gone wrong; and the scientific – that AIDS originated in African monkeys.

In 2001, the Royal Society of London's conference proceedings, which sought to determine the initial cause of AIDS and the origin of HIV, debated the possibility that HIV-1, the most widespread and deadly human AIDS virus, evolved from accidental vaccine contaminations and subsequent transmissions to mostly African villagers. The oral polio vaccine (OPV) was the focus of interest here since that vaccine was partially derived from growing live polio viruses in monkey kidney cells that have historically proven to be contaminated with cancer viruses such as SV40 – the fortieth monkey virus ever discovered – currently linked by medical scientists to widespread human cancers. By the end of the symposium, the esteemed delegates concluded that HIV/AIDS was unlikely to have originated from polio vaccine transmissions as chimpanzees were not proven to have been used during the manufacture of this vaccine.

In the same year, Gerald Myers – the US government's chief DNA sequence analyst – and his colleagues offered the following pre-eminent explanation for the origin of HIV. According to their report HIV could not have begun with single isolated cross-species transmissions because their genetic sequencing studies proved that some 'punctuated origin of AIDS event' took place during the mid-1970s, giving rise, virtually simultaneously, to at least ten different HIV 'clades' (or genetic subtypes) associated with ten different

---

Box 2.2 HIV subtypes

HIV has shown a remarkable ability to exploit and adapt to changes in the social environment. At the molecular level, also, the virus is constantly changing.

In order to map the genetic variation of HIV-1, scientists have classified different strains of the virus into three groups: M (main), O (outlier) and N (non-M, non-O).

The main group (M) is further classified into a number of subtypes, as well as variants resulting from the combination of two or more subtypes, known as 'circulating recombinant forms' (CRFs). Subtypes are defined as having genomes that are at least 25 per cent unique. Eleven subtypes have been identified and each is designated by a letter (subtype A or C and so on). When subtypes blend with each other (for example, when an individual is infected with two different HIV subtypes), and the resulting genetic blend successfully establishes itself in the environment, it is known as a CRF. So far, sixteen CRFs have been identified (Los Alamos National Laboratory, 2005).

To date, some subtypes have remained largely limited to certain geographic areas. Subtype C, for example, is widespread in southern Africa, India and Ethiopia. Subtype B is common in Europe, the Americas and Australia. But nearly all subtypes can be found in Africa, together with a number of CRFs.

---

distinguishable AIDS epidemics in Africa alone (box 2.2) (Burr et al., 2001). The most likely cause of this widespread bizarre zoonosis was some man-made (i.e. iatrogenic) event involving chimpanzees, this group reckoned. '[I]t is not far-fetched', they wrote,

> to imagine the ten or so clades deriving from a single animal (perhaps immunosuppressed and possessing a swarm of variants) [as might have been the case with chimpanzees used in

the process of vaccine manufacture] or from a few animals that might have belonged to a single troop or might have been gang-caged together. The number of animals required is secondary to the extent of variation in the source at the time of the zoonotic or iatrogenic event. The [vaccine] hypothesis makes a case for such a punctuated origin. (Burr et al., 2001, p. 884)

So if chimpanzees were not used to make the polio vaccine, and therefore HIV and AIDS did not come from this vaccine or this time period (1950s–early 1960s), then what other vaccine, given during the early to mid-1970s, might have used one or more infected chimpanzees in the manufacturing process? The answer to this question was singularly advanced by Leonard Horowitz in the award-winning book *Emerging Viruses: AIDS and Ebola – Nature, Accident or Intentional?* (1996). Horowitz unearthed and reprinted stunning scientific documents and National Institutes of Health contracts proving that chimpanzees, contaminated with numerous viruses, were used to produce hundreds of hepatitis B vaccine doses administered to central African blacks along with homosexual men in New York City at precisely the time Myers and colleagues claim the origin-of-HIV 'punctuated event' occurred.

Unfortunately, as another Royal Society conference presenter, Dr Julian Cribb, protested, too little attention is given by drug-industry-influenced medical journals, and the mainstream media, to controversial truths in science regarding the origin of HIV and AIDS (see Cribb, 2001). As a result, documents such as those published by Horowitz and others showing that AIDS apparently derives from contaminated hepatitis B vaccines have never received adequate attention. Attention, instead, has focused on Africa as the metaphysical prime suspect for bringing AIDS to the world. On the face of it, it is not difficult to see why: as noted earlier, by far the majority of countries affected by HIV/AIDS are in Africa, where the regional average HIV prevalence (among 15- to 49-year-olds) is 7.4 per cent (UNAIDS, 2004b). To place this in context, eight out of every ten people living with HIV/AIDS are Africans and the same proportion of new HIV infections is currently taking place in Africa. Since the predominant route of transmission in Africa is thought to be heterosexual intercourse, the inference has been drawn that hyper-sexuality allied with widespread promiscuity explains Africa's particular vulnerability to HIV/AIDS.

Though not always explicit, the presentation of hyper-sexualized societies in Africa, of course, was readily accepted because it tapped into a much deeper Western social consciousness. In much of the Western popular imagery the African continent has long been associated with all that is instinctive, primitive and sexual. Early European travellers, for example, returned from Africa bringing tales of black men allegedly performing carnal athletic feats with black women who were themselves sexually insatiable. The affront to Victorian sensibilities was cited alongside tribal conflicts and other 'uncivilized' behaviour to justify the need for colonial social control. In this context, the framing of African sexuality as the prime suspect behind the global HIV/AIDS epidemic is a convenient twist to an old meta-narrative. In truth, there is little proof to support this, and to date no evidence exists that shows that people from Botswana, Namibia, South Africa, Swaziland or any part of Africa are more sexually active than people from France, the United Kingdom, Germany, the United States or Japan. Moreover, the scientific community dismisses the notion that males from any continent or, indeed, region are more addicted to sex than those from another because testosterone levels, the measure of sexual vigour in men, never vary more than a tiny fraction of a percentage anywhere in the world.

What is in contention here is not that particular social patterns (including sexual behaviour) are exposing Africans to a greater risk of contracting the HIV virus – a point to which we shall return – but that there is something in the culture of Africa or in the sexual mores of its population which easily explains their plight. Clearly, sexual behaviour is an important factor in the transmission of sexually transmitted diseases. It alone, however, cannot explain why HIV prevalence is as high as 35 per cent of the adult population in some African countries and less than 1 per cent in the developed world.

HIV/AIDS Prevalence and Incidence

The most common measure of the HIV/AIDS epidemic is the *prevalence* of HIV infections among a country's adult population – in other words, the percentage of the adult population living with HIV. Prevalence of HIV provides a good picture of the overall *state* of the epidemic. Think of it as a still photograph of HIV/AIDS. In countries with generalized epidemics, this image is based largely on HIV tests done on anonymous blood samples taken from women attending antenatal clinics. But prevalence offers a less clear picture of recent *trends* in the epidemic, because it does not distinguish between people who acquired the virus very recently and those who were infected a decade or more ago. (Without antiretroviral treatment, a person might survive, on average, up to nine to eleven years after acquiring HIV; with treatment, survival is substantially longer.)

Countries A and B, for example, could have the same HIV prevalence, but be experiencing very different epidemics. In country A, the vast majority of people living with HIV/AIDS (the prevalent cases) might have been infected five to ten years ago, with few recent infections occurring. In country B, the majority of people living with HIV/AIDS might have been infected in the past two years. These differences would obviously have a huge impact on the kind of prevention and care efforts that countries A and B need to mount. Similarly, HIV prevalence rates might be stable in country C, suggesting that few new infections are occurring. That may not be the case, however. Country C could be experiencing higher rates of AIDS mortality (as people infected a decade or so ago die in large numbers) and an *increase* in new infections. The mortality offsetting the new infections gives the illusion of stable prevalence. Overall HIV prevalence rates would not illuminate those details of the country's epidemic.

So a measure of HIV *incidence* (i.e. the number of new infections observed over a year among previously uninfected people) would help complete the picture of current trends. Think of it as an animated image of the epidemic. The problem is that measuring HIV incidence is expensive and complicated – to the point of it being unfeasible at a national level and on a regular basis in most countries. None of this means, however, that recent trends are a mystery. Regular measurement of HIV prevalence among groups of young people can serve as a proxy, albeit imperfect, for HIV incidence among them. Because of their age, young people will have become infected relatively recently. Significant changes in HIV prevalence among 15- to 19- or 15- to 24-year-olds can therefore reflect important new trends in the epidemic.

Prevalence and Demographic Trends

Of the global total of just under 40 million persons living with HIV in 2004, around two-thirds (25.4 million) are in sub-Saharan Africa (see figure 2.1). HIV prevalence varies greatly by subregion, with the epidemic being at its most severe in southern and eastern Africa, and north and to some extent west Africa showing relatively low prevalence rates. Central Africa takes an intermediate position, but, as in all other subregions, with great variations between and within countries (see figure 2.2). These variations are so great that some argue that it is warranted to treat these as separate (although interlinked) epidemics.

Analysis of the trends in HIV prevalence over time show that the subregional variations in prevalence are not caused by the timing of the onset of the epidemic in that area, nor are they caused by the stage that the epidemic has reached (WHO-AFRO, 2003). Although far from fully understood, much has been learned over the past two decades about the epidemiological, demographic and behavioural aspects and

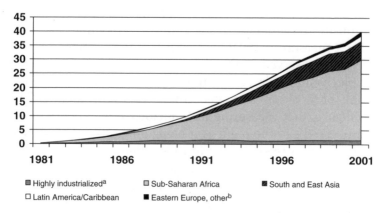

[a] North America, Europe (except Eastern Europe), Japan, Australia and New Zealand.
[b] Eastern Europe, Central Asia, Middle East and North Africa.
Sources: UN/DESA, 2005a; WHO-AFRO, 2003; and unpublished data

Figure 2.1 Growth of the AIDS epidemic: people with HIV/AIDS, cumulative regional totals (millions)

drivers of the HIV/AIDS pandemic in Africa. Particularly in the southern and eastern parts of the continent, a deadly combination of factors such as poverty, extensive work migration, gender inequity, low access to reproductive health care and the presence of other sexually transmitted infections (STIs) creates an enabling environment for HIV to spread. The mix of factors that further or hinder the spread of HIV is present to varying degrees in the different African subregions, creating different trajectories in them, although HIV/AIDS remains a devastating threat throughout the continent.

It follows that the cumulative affected population in Africa, taking into account spouses, children and elderly dependants, must be of the order of 235 million (28 million currently living with HIV plus 19 million who have died, multiplied by a factor of five to represent those directly affected). This is a staggering proportion of the total population in sub-Saharan Africa – almost one-third of Africans

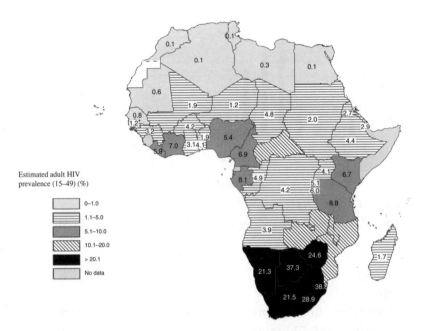

Source: CHGA using data from UNAIDS/WHO (UN/DESA, 2005b)

Figure 2.2 Geographical variation in HIV prevalence (per cent), end 2003

are directly affected by the HIV epidemic. Few people can remain unaffected in indirect ways, that is, through the illness and death of relatives, friends and in their workplaces and their communities.

Across the continent, infection is concentrated in the socially and economically productive groups aged 15–49, with more women infected than men. There are significant differences in the ages of infection of girls and boys, with infection occurring at younger ages for girls (with girls and young women in some countries outnumbering boys and young men by factors of five or six in the age range 15–20) – see figure 2.3. It is estimated that 24 million persons have died from HIV-related illnesses since the start of the

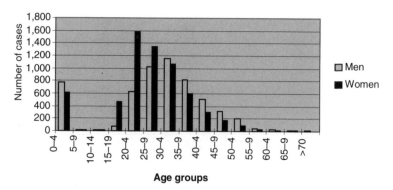

Source: CHGA, 2003

Figure 2.3 Typical age and sex distribution of AIDS cases in Africa

epidemic worldwide, of whom more than 19 million were Africans.

Especially in high-prevalence countries, the impact of HIV/AIDS on mortality, life expectancy and household structures is increasingly evident. Changes that are occurring include the following.

Increases in Mortality

Increases in mortality are particularly noticeable among young children and people 20 to 50 years of age. In South Africa, HIV/AIDS accounted for 40 per cent of all adult deaths in 2000–1, an increase from 10 per cent in 1995–6. In eastern and southern Africa, female mortality due to HIV/AIDS tends to occur five to ten years earlier than for men because women are generally infected at earlier ages. People in this age group are often described as at the prime of their productive years, working and raising families. Illness and death of adult members of a household reduce the ability of households to provide for themselves. Dependency ratios increase, as fewer adults are alive to care for children and the elderly. Increasingly, older members of extended families assume a greater role in caring for and supporting remaining family members. As important as an adult death is whether that person was a woman or a man. The loss of a male adult can leave the remaining women and children with fewer economic opportunities and less control over productive assets, including equipment and land. The loss of a female may result in increased malnutrition and generally less care for the children.

Declines in Life Expectancy

Declines in life expectancy follow as adults die at younger ages than would have been the case without HIV/AIDS. In many countries, HIV/AIDS is halting and indeed reversing many of the gains in life expectancy that have been enjoyed through continual improvements in health and education, reductions in poverty and economic growth. Currently, the average life expectancy in sub-Saharan Africa is 47 years. In the absence of AIDS, it would have been closer to 62 years. In Botswana, life expectancy at birth has dropped to a level not seen since before 1950, and in less than ten years many countries in the region will see life expectancies fall to near 30 years, levels not seen since the end of the nineteenth century. Figure 2.4 and table 2.1 illustrate changes (and projected changes) in life expectancy for selected African countries over a three-decade period. It is important to note that declines in life expectancy are not confined to the most severely affected countries. In Burkina Faso, where HIV prevalence was expected to reach 'only' about 10 per cent of adults in 2000, projections indicate that life expectancy will fall by ten to eleven years by 2010. The effects of HIV and AIDS are reflected in the changes in life expectancy, which is the best summary indicator of the effects of HIV and AIDS on countries with high levels of HIV prevalence. In many countries adult mortality has doubled and trebled over the past decade and this is directly attributable to HIV and AIDS. These data are remarkable for what they illustrate of the demographic impact of the epidemic on African populations.

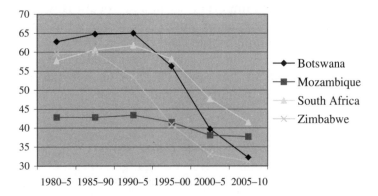

Source: Data from UN Population Division, 2003
Figure 2.4 Changes in life expectancy in four countries, 1980–5 to 2005–10

Differing Male/Female Infection Rates

A 2000 survey in Bobo-Dioulasso, Burkina Faso, showed that infection rates among young girls aged 13 to 24 were between five and eight times higher than those among boys of the same age. In Zimbabwe and Zambia, surveys show that prevalence levels among young women are three to four times higher than among young men (see figure 2.5).

In lower-prevalence situations, young men usually have higher infection rates than young women; as the pandemic progresses, an increasing number of women are infected. Females have higher infection rates at an earlier age than males for a combination of both socio-economic (e.g. gender discrimination in schooling, jobs access and wage rates, greater difficulty in accessing preventive and curative health care) and biological reasons (e.g. susceptibility to vaginal infections and abrasions, particularly at young ages) (see box 2.3).

Redistribution of Population

Because AIDS deaths are most heavily concentrated among women and men 20 to 50 years of age, the classic

Table 2.1 Loss of life expectancy at birth due to AIDS by sex in the seven countries with the highest adult HIV prevalence, 2000–5, 2010–15 and 2020–5

Country	Loss of life expectancy at birth due to AIDS (years)		Percentage difference between life expectancy with and without AIDS	
	Male	Female	Male	Female
2000–5				
Botswana	27.5	29.1	41	42
Lesotho	25.1	22.8	44	38
Namibia	20.6	21.6	32	32
South Africa	17.9	19.7	28	28
Swaziland	26.6	29.1	44	45
Zambia	19.0	23.1	37	42
Zimbabwe	32.1	36.9	49	53
2010–15				
Botswana	35.6	42.3	52	58
Lesotho	29.3	32.3	48	50
Namibia	26.5	32.2	40	45
South Africa	24.7	32.2	37	44
Swaziland	32.8	38.9	51	57
Zambia	19.8	24.6	36	42
Zimbabwe	35.5	42.0	52	58
2020–25				
Botswana	34.3	42.5	48	57
Lesotho	29.3	34.6	45	51
Namibia	25.6	31.8	37	43
South Africa	23.3	31.1	34	42
Swaziland	32.9	39.7	49	56
Zambia	20.2	25.6	34	40
Zimbabwe	33.9	41.9	48	56

Source: Data from UN/DESA, 2005a

Box 2.3 Why are young African women
so vulnerable to HIV infection?

Despite recent positive trends among young people (especially females) in some African countries, overall about twice as many young women as men are infected in sub-Saharan Africa. In 2001, an estimated 6–11 per cent of young women aged 15–24 were living with HIV/AIDS, compared to 3–6 per cent of young men. This appears to be due to a combination of factors.

Women and girls are commonly discriminated against in terms of access to education, employment, credit, health care, land and inheritance. With the downward trend of many African economies increasing the numbers of people in poverty, relationships with men (casual or formalized through marriage) can serve as vital opportunities for financial and social security, or for satisfying material aspirations. Generally, older men are more likely to be able to offer such security. But, in areas where HIV/AIDS is widespread, they are also more likely to have become infected with HIV. The combination of dependence and subordination can make it very difficult for girls and women to demand safer sex (even from their husbands) or to end relationships that carry the threat of infection.

Studies have shown that young women tend to marry men several years older, and that their risk of infection increases if a husband is three or more years older than they are. Meanwhile, ignorance about sexual and reproductive health and HIV/AIDS is widespread. In countries with generalized epidemics in Africa, up to 80 per cent of women aged 15–24 have been shown to lack sufficient knowledge about HIV/AIDS. This, combined with the fact that young women and girls are more biologically prone to infection (the cervix being susceptible to lesions), helps explain the large differences in HIV prevalence between girls and boys aged 15–19.

Source: CHGA, 2004b

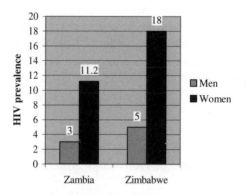

Source: Data from WHO-AFRO, 2003
Figure 2.5 Gender differences in prevalence among youth (per cent)

population pyramid is projected to morph into a 'population chimney'. Infant and child mortality will increase, as will mortality in the age brackets of people 20 to 50 years old. In Botswana and elsewhere, young women will die at a younger age than young men, reflecting the earlier age at which women are infected. This may increase social tensions and gender violence as fewer younger women are available for partnering with young men. At the same time, it may give young women greater control over relationships as they may have greater flexibility in the choices of men they wish to be with.

Decreases in Population Growth

In Côte d'Ivoire, it is estimated that the population growth rate will decrease by about 0.5 per cent per year as a result of HIV/AIDS. According to one assessment, the slowing down of the growth of the population means that by the end of 2007, Côte d'Ivoire will have around one and a half million fewer people than it otherwise would have had. This will be as a result of two factors: first, increased mortality as a result of AIDS; and, second, decreased fertility (fewer people of reproductive age, lower sexual activity among PLWHA). In Botswana, South Africa, Lesotho, Swaziland and Zimbabwe, the growth rate is expected to become negative by 2015. In the absence of AIDS, the countries would have had growth rates of 1.5–2 per cent by that year (UN/DESA, 2005a).

Changes in Household Structures

As indicated above, households will change, with more female-, child- and elderly-headed households. Some households, however, will dissolve completely, either because of economic destitution or because of the death of parents and dispersal of children. Projections done in Botswana suggest that nearly 7 per cent of all households – particularly small households – will disappear by 2008.

Increase in the Number of Orphans

It is estimated that there are presently some 12.3 million children in Africa who have lost one or both parents to HIV-related illnesses, and by 2010 these numbers are projected to increase to some 18.4 million. The most severely affected countries in terms of AIDS orphans in 2003 were Nigeria (1.8 million), South Africa (1.1 million), Tanzania (980,000), Zimbabwe (980,000), Uganda (940,000), Democratic Republic of the Congo (770,000), Ethiopia (720,000), Kenya (650,000), Zambia (630,000) and Malawi (500,000) (UNICEF/UNAIDS/USAID, 2004). These are truly staggering numbers. In some countries the proportion of all children under 15 years of age who have lost one or both parents to AIDS may be as high as 20 per cent, possibly even higher, by the end of the first decade of the new millennium. It should be noted that AIDS orphans account for only a proportion of the total number of orphans from all causes, so that the overall problem is even more serious. The most recent estimate is that the total number of orphans in Africa in 2010 will be 50 million, of whom 37 per cent will be AIDS orphans (UNICEF/UNAIDS/USAID, 2004). These trends have direct implications for intergenerational poverty and impose immense challenges for policy makers.

The Worst is Yet to Come

Because of the five- to ten-years time lag between infection and the onset of HIV-related illness and death, the impact felt today is a result of past levels of prevalence. Present prevalence levels will only translate into morbidity and mortality a few years down the line. In the absence of widespread, effective mitigation, it is chilling to note that the worst of the impact is therefore yet to come.

The Core Drivers of Africa's HIV/AIDS Crisis

Spanning from the structural to the individual level, the determinants of Africa's HIV/AIDS crisis include factors such as governance and culture, health care infrastructure and women's legal rights, sexual norms and mixing patterns, down to proximate determinants such as presence of other sexually transmitted infections or the virus subtype. Figure 2.6 summarizes and categorizes these factors.

The rest of this section will discuss some of the core drivers of Africa's HIV/AIDS epidemic under the following four broad headings: biological; socio-cultural; socio-economic; and socio-political/historical. A word of caution, however, must be entered once again here because the evidence is quite mixed with respect to the extent to which each of these groups of factors contribute to the spread and entrenchment of the pandemic across the continent.

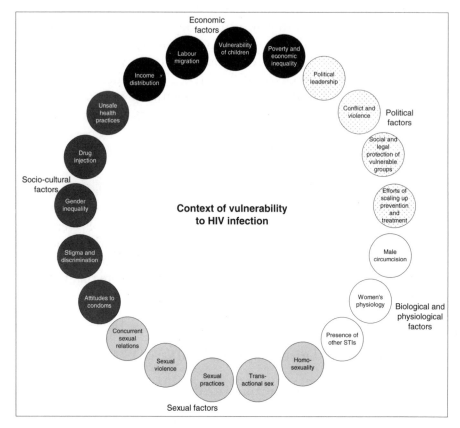

Figure 2.6 Fuelling factors

Biological Factors

On the biological front, research points to three key factors as the proximate determinants of Africa's high HIV infectivity. The first of these is the existence of undiagnosed and untreated sexually transmitted diseases among many Africans. Data for 2000 indicate that Africa has the highest incidence of curable STDs at 284 cases per 1,000 people aged 15–49 years, compared to the second highest of 160 cases per 1,000 people in South and South-East Asia. There is now growing recognition of the public health implications of curable STDs (especially those causing genital ulcers) by virtue of their frequency of occurrence as well as their ability, when present, to facilitate the transmission of HIV (World Bank, 2000b). One study suggests that the presence of an untreated STD can increase the risk of both the acquisition and transmission of HIV by a factor of up to ten (MEDILINKS, 2001). Such painful bacterial STDs are relatively uncommon in rich countries because of the availability of antibiotics. Yet in Africa, even when the poor have access to health care, the clinics may have no antibiotics to treat those bacterial STDs that act as co-factors for HIV.

One biological factor that has emerged in the recent literature as having some influence on the spread and transmission of HIV is the low rate of male circumcision found in some African countries. However, it should be pointed out here that there are a much higher proportion of both males and females who are circumcised in Africa than in any other continent (Caldwell et al., 2000). Nonetheless, in the main AIDS belt in Africa (east and southern Africa), there is a strong association between the high incidence of the disease and the lack of male circumcision. In these geographic locations, entire ethnic groups do not practise male circumcision and the epidemiological analysis strongly suggests that the 'lack of circumcision either directly facilitates HIV transmission and/or facilitates it by rendering chancroid and other GUD [genital ulcerating disease] infections more likely' (Caldwell, 1995; Caldwell et al., 2000). Indeed, a review of more than twenty-five published studies on the association between HIV and male circumcision in Africa found that, on average, circumcised men were half as likely to be infected with HIV as uncircumcised men. Moreover, a comparison of African men with similar socio-demographic, behavioural and other factors found that circumcised men were nearly 60 per cent less likely than uncircumcised men to be infected with HIV (Caldwell et al., 2000).

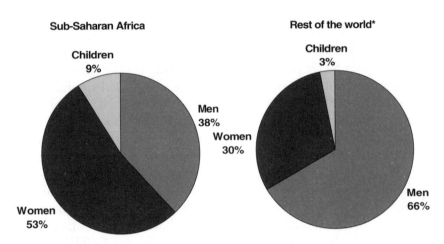

Sub-Saharan Africa   Rest of the world*

* Total does not equal 100 per cent due to rounding.
Source: Data from UNAIDS, 2004b
Figure 2.7 Composition of people living with HIV/AIDS, 2004

The second biological factor to be considered here pertains to the physiological vulnerability of women. Research shows that the risk of becoming infected with HIV during unprotected vaginal intercourse is as much as two to four times higher for women of all ages than for men. Women are also much more vulnerable to other STDs. In sub-Saharan Africa, there are currently six women with HIV for every five men and more than four-fifths of the global total of HIV-infected women are African – (see figure 2.7). In the younger age brackets (15–24 years), the HIV risk for African girls is even more disproportionate as young women outnumber their male peers by ratio of 2 to 1 in those countries where young people account for 60 per cent of all new infections (Lurie et al., 2003b; UNAIDS, 2004b). In comparison to men, women are biologically more vulnerable to HIV infection due to the fact that they have a bigger surface area of mucosa exposed to their partner's sexual secretions during sexual intercourse, and semen infected with HIV typically contains a higher concentration of virus than a woman's sexual secretions. All of this makes the male-to-female transmission much more efficient than the female-to-male transmission. In addition, the younger a woman is, the greater is her biological risk since her physiologically immature cervix and sparse vaginal secretions pose less of a barrier to HIV.

Socio-cultural Factors

Alongside the biological factors are a number of sociobehavioural factors which either are regarded as having or have been demonstrated to have a major impact on the transmission of HIV/AIDS in Africa. These factors tend to be derived from traditions and practices. Take the issue of multipartner relationships. In most African societies, many people either do not, or cannot, limit their sexual activities to a single, infection-free lifetime partner (Schoepf, 1993). Indeed, there exists a rather significant literature with empirical evidence on polygynous relationships and multi-partner sexual relations and their implications for the spread of HIV/AIDS (Hope and Gaborone, 1999). The high levels of polygyny and the system it engenders have serious implications for the spread of the AIDS epidemic since entire families may find themselves as victims of the disease through polygynous association. In part, because farming and economic viability depend solely on the size of the workforce, sub-Saharan Africa is characterized by very high levels of polygyny.

According to Hope (2001), some 30–50 per cent of married women in Africa are currently in polygynous marriages. This state of affairs means that, for these women, the greatest danger of infection confronting them comes from their spouses, and it is most likely that the majority of female AIDS victims have been infected by their husbands (Caldwell et al., 1993; Orubuloye and Caldwell, 1997). At the same time, however, there is evidence from some African communities that since the husband could only serve one wife at a time, polygyny does not provide co-wives with adequate sexual pleasure, leaving the others neglected and tempted to seek alternative lovers. On the other hand, some young women might accept polygynous marriages to be able to acquire some degree of economic status, while at the same time maintaining their previous sexual relationships (Mbilinyi and Kaihula, 2000). In all of the foregoing scenarios, polygynous marriages endanger the lives of those associated with them.

Apart from polygynous relationships, multi-partner sexual relations are also prevalent in Africa through sexual networking. Sexual networking is characterized by the prevalence of multiple (overlapping or concurrent) sexual partnerships. In particular, men's sexual networks seem to be quite extensive and appear to be accepted, at least tacitly, by the society at large. In many African countries, there is a general feeling that men may legitimately have multiple relationships, irrespective of their marital status, but women may not. This attitude is justified on the basis of culture. A study conducted in Nigeria, for example, found that the need for men to have sexual variation, and the assumed polygynous nature of man, were the two main reasons why men cannot be satisfied with one woman. It is generally believed that men are biologically different from women in their need for sex and, as such, should have unlimited sexual freedom while a woman is expected to have only one partner (Orubuloye et al., 1993). Consequently, these high and repeated levels of infidelity render women more likely than men to be put at risk of HIV by their partner's sexual encounters. The consequences for a woman who remains faithful to an unfaithful partner can therefore be devastating. She not only finds herself at risk but also risks infecting her future children.

HIV/AIDS is linked to sex, blood and death – issues that are culturally difficult to handle, often taboo and stigmatized. The introduction of HIV as an 'immoral' disease in early prevention programmes has probably contributed significantly to the HIV-associated stigma observed today. Stigma increases discrimination and marginalization, and increases vulnerability to HIV infection as well as increasing the consequences once infected through several paths. Fearful of discrimination, individuals at high risk of contracting HIV may stay away from information and prevention services. Governments may stop prevention programmes that promote condom use, or that aim to provide sexuality-related education for youth. Fear of stigmatization and discrimination keep those suspecting that they are infected from seeking information, advice, testing, support and other services. Numerous programmes seek to address stigma, but have so far not proven very effective. There is emerging evidence, however, that widespread testing coupled with provision of treatment decreases stigma as HIV/AIDS gradually becomes a disease like any other.

Socio-economic Factors

The struggle to survive every day overshadows attention and concern about a virus that does not demonstrate any immediate harm. In this sense, although the relationship between poverty and HIV transmission is not simple, it is possible that all the factors predisposing Africans – particularly girls and women – to increased risk of HIV infection are aggravated by poverty (Farmer et al., 1996; Kim et al., 2000; Namposya-Serpell, 2000; Sachs, 2001). The following examples will perhaps suffice to indicate how poverty leads to outcomes which expose the poor to a higher probability of contracting HIV. Poverty – especially rural poverty – and the absence of access to sustainable livelihoods are factors in labour mobility. Mobile workers are defined as those workers who work far away from their permanent places of residence and are usually unable to return home at the end of the working day. They therefore have temporary residences in the vicinity of their work sites and return home at various intervals. Such workers include, for example, truck drivers, road/dam/building construction workers, itinerant traders, soldiers, wildlife officers, seafarers, agricultural workers, miners and commercial sex workers. For these workers, being mobile in and of itself is not a risk factor for HIV/AIDS; it is the situations they encounter and the behaviours in which they may engage while they are travelling around that lead to and increase vulnerability to HIV/AIDS. Structural factors have led to some African regions, such as southern Africa, experiencing higher concentrations of migrant workers. This has present-day economic, but also historical, reasons, as the mode of land exploitation has taken the form of large commercial farms which require the hiring of migratory farm labour. Vast numbers of men have migrated to work in the numerous mines located in southern Africa.

Decosas and Adrien (1997) note that migrants have higher infection rates than those who do not migrate, independent of the HIV prevalence at the site of departure or the site of destination. The mining community in Carletonville, South Africa, is a tragic and powerful reminder of how mobility provides an environment of extraordinary risk for HIV contraction. With a mine-working population of 85,000 people, of whom 95 per cent are migrant workers, Carletonville is the biggest gold-mining complex in the world. These migrant workers leave their families behind in rural villages, live in squalid all-male labour hostels and return home maybe once a year. Lacking formal education and recreation, these hardworking men rely on little else but home-brewed alcohol and sex for leisure. For these men, there is a one in forty chance of being crushed by falling rock, so the delayed risk of HIV seems comparatively remote. Astonishingly, some 65 per cent of adults in Carletonville were HIV-positive in 1999, a rate higher than any region in the world (Williams et al., 2000). When these men return back to their families, they often carry the virus into their rural communities. A study in a rural area in the South African province of KwaZulu-Natal, for example, showed that 13 per cent of women whose husbands worked away from home two-thirds of the time or over were infected with HIV (Morar et al., 1998). Among women who spent two-thirds of their time or more with their husbands, no HIV infection was recorded (Lurie et al., 2003a). Mobility may also reduce risk by increasing access to information,

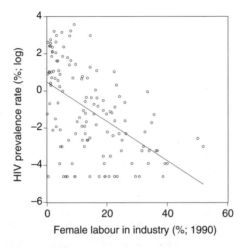

Source: Bonnel, 2000
Figure 2.8 Female employment and HIV prevalence rate

preventive practices, services and care. The UN Population Division reports that studies in Senegal, Uganda and Tanzania found that mobile individuals were more likely to report condom use than their non-mobile counterparts. It therefore seems that exposure to new environments need not automatically lead to risky behaviour if adequate support networks are in place (UN/DESA, 2005a).

To the extent that poverty prevents access to medical care, it facilitates the spread of HIV/AIDS. However, what seems more important than poverty is the extent to which there is a large socio-economic gap between women and men. HIV prevalence rates are lower when women have significant economic opportunities for remaining financially independent (figure 2.8), and when females have access to schooling (figure 2.9). Inequality (measured by the Gini coefficient) seems to be related to the HIV/AIDS prevalence rate. There is some indication that the larger the inequality, the greater the chance of a higher HIV prevalence (figure 2.10).

Poverty structures not only the contours of the pandemic but also the outcome once an individual is sick with

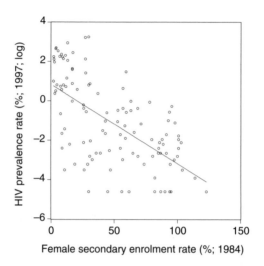

Source: Bonnel, 2000
Figure 2.9 HIV and female education

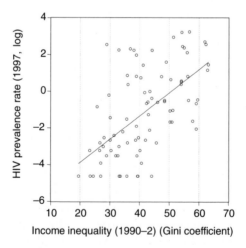

Source: Bonnel, 2000
Figure 2.10 Inequality and HIV prevalence rate

complications of HIV infection. A strong feature of HIV infection is that it clusters within families, often resulting in both parents being HIV positive – and in time falling sick and dying. Poor families have a reduced capacity to deal with the effects of morbidity and mortality compared to richer ones, for very obvious reasons. These include the absence of savings and other assets that can cushion the impact of illness and death. The poor are already on the margins of survival, and are unable to deal with the costs associated with HIV/AIDS. These include the cost of drugs – when available – to treat opportunistic infections, the cost of transport to health centres, reduced household productivity through illness and diversion of labour to caring roles, loss of employment through illness and job discrimination, funeral and related costs, and so on. In the longer term such poor households never recover even their initial level of living, since their capacity is reduced through the loss of productive family members through death and migration, and through the sales of any productive assets they once possessed. As a result, a true process of immiseration is now observable in many parts of Africa, particularly southern Africa. Take this powerful image from a field-worker in Zambia:

> In the field you are often led into somebody's home. The first thing that hits you is that the patient will be on the floor. If that household was not poor before HIV/AIDS infected somebody, then by the end of the first few years, poverty will come to the household as all of their assets are sold off to pay for healthcare. Children have been taken out of school – daughters, particularly – to become caregivers. Invariably, the person you have come to see will be on the floor without a blanket or a pillow. If you look around that mud hut for food, you won't see it, and you won't smell people cooking. There is no food. (Poku and Whiteside, 2004, p. 42)

There is thus enormous strain on the capacity of families to cope with the psychosocial and economic consequences of illness, such that many families experience great distress and often disintegrate as social and economic units. Even where they do not, by eliminating the breadwinners – often both parents – the process further exposes the rest of the family members to poverty, which then increases their chances of contracting the virus. This is particularly so for young women, who will often be forced to engage in commercial sexual transactions, sometimes as casual sex workers, as a survival strategy for themselves and their dependants (Greener et al., 2000; Machipisa, 2001; Mutangadura, 2000).

Socio-political and Historical Factors

Political and historical factors structure the environment in which the individual makes decisions concerning his or her everyday life, and are important as they can either bolster resistance or create vulnerability to HIV infection. Three such factors will be mentioned here.

The first is that lack of adequate investment in health infrastructure has made it much more difficult to provide adequate medical care and to prevent the spread of STIs, which is often mentioned as one of the co-factors of HIV/AIDS. AIDS especially affects the health sector because it reduces the supply of medical staff, and it increases the demand for AIDS-related medical services. As a result, it worsens the capacity of the health sector to treat other diseases, which leads to a worsening of the health status of the whole population.

A second such factor is the presence of conflict. Africa's borders have been drawn by former colonial powers on the basis of various political objectives rather than on the basis of national identities. This has led to a range of conflicts, which have facilitated the spread of HIV. Conflict is expensive – the World Health Organization estimates that Africa loses $15 billion every year due to conflict, diverting scarce resources from other pressing needs (Commission on Macroeconomics and Health, 2004). Furthermore, soldiers have been found to have high rates of HIV infection, and low access to HIV prevention interventions. Widespread rape, sexual abuse, as well as risky sex perpetrated by soldiers, mean that the presence of soldiers (including for peace-keeping purposes) represents a risk factor in communities. Populations fleeing armed conflict typically face very difficult conditions that increase the risk of contracting infections such as HIV. Traditional sexual norms and mechanisms of social control may break down, poverty is exacerbated, while access to health services and prevention (particularly condoms) is constrained (UN/DESA, 2005a). However, the impact of conflict can vary from setting to setting. For example, in Sierra Leone and Angola, conflict may have prevented extensive contact with outsiders, also preventing HIV from spreading.

A third factor is incarceration. While little is known about the spread of HIV in African prisons, prisoners generally hail from populations that are marginalized and therefore more at risk from HIV before they enter the prison – and conditions within the prison itself may facilitate further spread. One South African study found that HIV prevalence in prisons is twice as high as that of the population at large (Goyer, 2001).

Finally, a key factor explaining why some countries have been able to mount an effective response to the HIV/AIDS epidemic early on is whether governments are accountable to the broad majority of the population rather than to a narrow urban-based elite. From this perspective, Africa would seem to be lagging, which has made it much more difficult for AIDS-related issues to be translated into budgetary allocation decisions.

Concluding Remarks

It is increasingly clear that to address HIV/AIDS means to address the whole range of development challenges that the continent faces. Many of the conditions that facilitate the spread of HIV/AIDS are linked to low levels of development, poorly developed health infrastructure, lack of economic

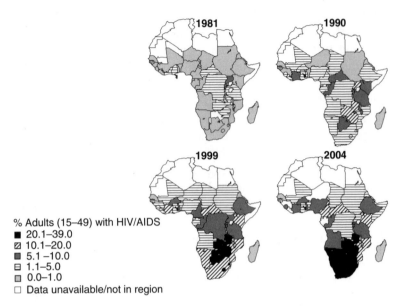

% Adults (15–49) with HIV/AIDS
- ■ 20.1–39.0
- ▨ 10.1–20.0
- ▣ 5.1 –10.0
- ⊟ 1.1–5.0
- ▢ 0.0–1.0
- ☐ Data unavailable/not in region

Source: Data from UNAIDS and UN/DESA (unpublished)
Figure 2.11 Map of HIV prevalence in sub-Saharan Africa, 1981–2004

empowerment, and so on. However, efforts to address HIV/AIDS so far have mainly been concentrated on prevention, and prevention has mainly focused on individual behaviour change. 'Education for prevention' programmes aimed at youth, commercial sex workers and both rural and urban populations have been implemented. The presumption that high rates of partner change explain the very high rates of HIV in Africa is generally not explicit in such prevention programmes. However, it is the implicit assumption behind an AIDS prevention policy that consists of behaviour modification and condom provision, with some recent attention to STIs. This notwithstanding, as figure 2.11 clearly illustrates, the concentration on behaviour modification that has informed this first generation of intervention strategies has not seriously affected the cause, intensity or direction of the pandemic in Africa.

One reason for this lack of impact might well be a fun-damental misunderstanding of the context of behaviour modification in societies. It is possible that sexual behaviour is not merely a matter of individual choice, but is predicated on society's sexual norms and values, economic relationships and the existence or lack of an environment that promotes the possibility of open and honest discussion of sexuality and dying. As such, any changes expected in societies' sexual behaviour must be based on an evolutionary process and expectations must be calibrated accordingly. Of course, in the context of HIV/AIDS there is an obvious disjuncture between the pace and intensity of the prevalence rates and the evolutionary processes involved in societies' sexual norms. As a result, it would – at first glance – appear that behaviour modification strategies are not working to stem the spread of the HIV/AIDS epidemic in Africa. This is certainly true of ABC – abstinence, behaviour change and condoms – which has come to dominate so many of the prevention programmes.

The problem with an 'ABC' approach is that the neat alphabetic label is only a beginning. It confuses the outcomes of successful HIV programmes with the message needed to achieve effective results. It also ignores the strong possibility that each of these components may be more or less effective or relevant depending on cultural, political and economic circumstances and the stage of the epidemic – early or late. Abstinence, fidelity or condom use are the successful out-comes of any behaviour change strategy for HIV/AIDS. We have known this since HIV was identified as a sexually trans-mitted infection, and these are proven goals for all STI pre-vention. But what is less well understood is how to bring about A, B and C.

The experience of Uganda is instructive. In its earliest responses, the government encouraged people to talk about HIV and AIDS and the result was a diversity of response. Of course, all who engage with the challenge of HIV/AIDS wish there were a 'magic bullet', a simple solution that could get people to change their behaviour. But sexual behaviour is precisely not simple. It is not even always mainly about what people may most immediately think of as 'sex'. It is tied up in complex ways with people's diverse life situations, with property, kinship alliance, ritual and religious beliefs, ancestors and gender relations, income and inequality, land and livelihoods.

3
The Socio-economic Impact of HIV/AIDS

Introduction

By the late 1990s, many governments and major international donors reacted to the growing evidence of the impact of HIV/AIDS on African households by suggesting that 'traditional' coping mechanisms would minimize the impact and allow households and communities to absorb the loss of members and of their income, assets and social contributions. This belief had an important political dimension. By acknowledging this element of African societies' traditional strengths, governments and international agencies were not obligated to respond to the multiple crises they faced as a critical emergency. As the impact of the epidemic has deepened and broadened, however, new research suggests that these broad generalizations about the impact of HIV/AIDS must be supported with credible evidence and qualified in particular circumstances. The slow evolution of the impact of HIV/AIDS does disguise the immediate general effects, but the cumulative effects registered over several years or one or two decades are already producing, and will continue to produce, significant changes across society.

What makes the HIV/AIDS epidemic worse than other epidemics is that it is slow-acting. In the case of 'traditional' epidemics, the early increase in death has the benefit of mobilizing efforts early on to control the epidemic. As a result, the development effects of such epidemics are usually limited to the short term. In the case of HIV/AIDS, there is no similar pressure to mount a strong public health campaign at an early stage because the disease remains invisible for many years. During this time, the infection has succeeded in spreading throughout the population. When action is finally launched, the epidemic has reached the AIDS stage, and it is usually too late to avoid its economic and development impacts (see figure 3.1). This chapter outlines the major impacts of HIV/AIDS on the social and economic structures in sub-Saharan Africa. The evidence used in the chapter reflects the current state of research and analysis. In some instances, the evidence might be called 'best practices'. In other instances, the evidence is still emerging, and clear directions remain to be further explored.

The Impacts of HIV/AIDS on Families and Communities

A degree of caution is necessary when assessing the impact of HIV/AIDS on households and communities because other factors are at work at the same time. Dramatic economic changes in sub-Saharan Africa over the past several decades, for example, have left some households more exposed to the impact of HIV/AIDS than others. Households and communities already suffering conditions of poverty are, usually, most harmed by the loss of adult members to illnesses, including HIV/AIDS. Female- and elderly-headed households are likewise least able to cope with the economic, labour and social losses arising from HIV/AIDS. Thus, if we want to know whether households are coping with the impact of HIV/AIDS, we need to include the wider socio-economic context in the analysis *and* identify who is most affected. Differentiation of data by gender, age and socio-economic status is critical.

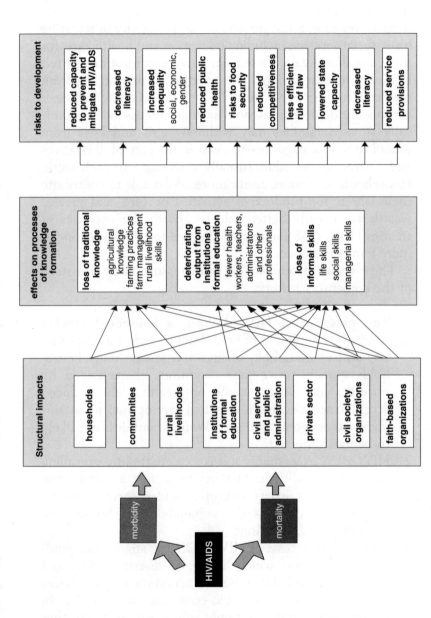

Figure 3.1 The impact of HIV/AIDS on development

Another parallel change to the prevailing poverty in many societies, more directly associated with structural-adjustment-induced reforms, is the greater cost and difficulty in accessing basic social services, including education and health care, for many families. Again, these costs have been most deeply felt by lower income groups. The additional costs arising from medical care for people with HIV/AIDS and related illnesses can readily deplete household savings and assets. Economically stressed families may withdraw girls and boys from school to reduce expenses, to assist in the care of ill relatives and to free up an adult (usually a woman) to seek work. Households with more assets, more adults able to contribute their labour for productive activities or care, and greater wealth are usually better able to absorb the expenses of treating HIV/AIDS and related illnesses and the loss of one or more family members.

Three broad statements do seem reasonable at this stage of the epidemic's history:

1 The presence of HIV/AIDS in a household quickly results in a depletion of household income-earning capacity and of household savings and assets. Many households quickly move into conditions characterized by poverty: very little income or wealth, debt, reduced access to services, and fewer than ever options for attaining socio-economic security. Women and girls are likely to be most affected.

2 HIV/AIDS exacerbates and is exacerbated by prevailing economic conditions. HIV/AIDS is not a stand-alone condition, but exists within a wider socio-economic context that deepens the vulnerability of households, communities and nations.

3 The economic costs of HIV/AIDS, the stigma surrounding the disease, which leads to discrimination and withdrawal, and difficulties in accessing social services combine to expand socio-economic inequalities in society. HIV/AIDS is not only killing people, it is further dividing national societies.

Table 3.1 illustrates the possible pathways of HIV/AIDS impacts on families and communities. The first and greatest impact is at the level of individuals and households. Whiteside (2002) rightly makes the observation that 'macro-economic impact takes longer to evolve and the scale and magnitude of macro-impact will depend on the scale and location of micro-level impacts' (p. 314). Household-level and community-level impacts are most serious but there are few data about them. From the limited household studies we can draw the following conclusions: first, the impact of adult illness and death and the way households cope suggest that individuals and households go through processes of experimentation and adaptation as they cope with immediate and long-term demographic changes – see table 3.2 (Barnett and Blaikie, 1992; Drinkwater, 1993). Over a five-year period one episode of illness may be followed by others which gradually deplete the resources and labour of one or more interdependent households. A study in the Kagera region of Tanzania showed movements of households or family members into and out of the household within six months prior to and soon after death, and these changes were identified to have an important role in household coping strategies (Bond and Wallman, 1993; Donahue, 1998).

Second, the effect of illness and death on poverty in households depends on the number of cases the household experiences; the characteristics of deceased individuals; the household's composition and asset array; community attitudes towards helping needy households and the general availability of resources – the level of life – in that community; and the broader resources available for assistance to households. In other words, the poorer the households and communities, the worse the impact.

These household observations confirm the fact that morbidity and mortality are putting enormous strain on the capacity of families to cope with the psycho-social and economic consequences of illness, such that many families experience great distress and often disintegrate as social and economic units (Poku, 2003). The precise nature of these

Table 3.1 Impact of HIV/AIDS at the household level

Production and earnings	Investment and consumption	Household health and composition	Psycho-social costs
Reduced income	Medical costs	Health maintenance activities reduced	Loss of individual motivation
Reduced productivity	Funeral costs	Loss of individual motivation	Grief of survivors
		Loss of deceased	
Reduced labour use of land	Legal fees	Poor health of survivors	
	Loss of savings	Dissolution of household	
	Changes in consumption and investment		

Table 3.2 The three stages of loss management

Stages	Loss management strategies
Reversible mechanisms and disposal of self-insuring assets	Seeking wage labour or migrating temporarily to find work
	Switching to producing low-maintenance subsistence food crops (which are usually less nutritious)
	Liquidating savings
	Tapping obligations from extended family or community members
	Soliciting family or marriage remittance
	Borrowing from formal or informal sources of credit
	Reducing consumption
Disposal of productive assets	Selling land, equipment or tools
	Borrowing at exorbitant interest rates
	Further reducing consumption, education or health expenditure
	Reducing amount of land farmed or crops produced
Destitution	Depending on charity
	Breaking up households
	Distress migration

Source: Donahue, 1998

disintegrations is something we know very little about – a point to which we shall return. Similarly, there is no literature on the implications of the process of fragmentation for the survival or maintenance of deeply affected communities. Evidently, countries are living with high numbers of HIV/AIDS cases in their communities and the fact that people are not dying on streets would suggest that they are coping. Yet we are also witnessing family break-ups and their members – orphans, widows and the elderly – joining other households. As such, the notion of 'coping' has to be questioned in relation to the systematic intergenerational implications of HIV/AIDS.

The Burden of Care

Women and girls tend to provide most of the care for sick individuals, but men do play an important (albeit less full) role, especially in the care of other men. Also, the differences in the time spent on care between women and men may not be as great as sometimes assumed, although the evidence is incomplete. A survey of households affected by HIV/AIDS in several provinces of South Africa found that in more than two-thirds of households women or girls were the primary caregivers (CHGA, 2004a). Almost a quarter of caregivers (23 per cent) were over the age of 60 and just under three-quarters of these were women. Similar findings were seen in Zimbabwe. There, most people caring for children orphaned by HIV/AIDS were over 50 years of age. Of those, over 70 per cent were 60 years or older. The stress of caregiving was clear. Caregivers report regular concerns about adequate food and clothing, the high cost of medical fees and inability to pay school fees for orphans. Indeed, the health of the older caregivers had deteriorated as a result of the physical and emotional stress of assisting the children.

The burden of care on households is significant. A study of urban and rural households in the South African Free State Province found that caregivers devoted four hours a day to caring for sick relatives, plus the time taken to accompany a sick relative to a health facility (Kelly, 2001). Interestingly, for most caregivers, the assistance they provided came on top of regular work. When a person became terminally ill, the time devoted to care nearly doubled, to 7.5 hours per day. A household survey in Côte d'Ivoire found no respondents with AIDS hospitalized over the four months of the last survey round, indicating that care was provided at home (Desmond et al., 2000). Further, urban-based relatives often return to a rural home, when they become too sick to work or care for themselves, thereby shifting primary caregiving to family members. On the other hand, some rural-based civil servants apply for transfers to urban posts when they become ill, so as to be closer to medical facilities.

Caregiving involves opportunity costs. In South Africa, 40 per cent of caregivers took time off from work or income-generating activities (Steinberg et al., 2002). Children took time off from school or studying to provide care. Food production and household chores all suffered in lieu of caregiving in 60 per cent of affected households.

Orphaned Children

As young and middle-aged adults die of HIV/AIDS, hundreds of thousands of children are orphaned. The growing number of orphaned children is most evident in southern and eastern Africa (see figure 3.2), but such girls and boys can be found wherever HIV/AIDS is present. In sub-Saharan Africa, an estimated 11 million children had lost their mothers or both parents as of 2001; the number is expected to climb to 20 million by 2010 (Save the Children UK, 2002). By that date, too, it is estimated that 75 per cent of all orphanhood in Zambia, Swaziland and Namibia will be due to AIDS. Though the absolute numbers are important, perhaps more important is the speed at which the numbers are increasing, indicating the mushrooming pressures on households, communities, government services and civil society to address the needs of orphaned children. Local community leaders regularly report that their groups are overwhelmed by the number of orphaned children they find and who need various forms of assistance.

In addition to the daily care of people ill with HIV/AIDS or related illnesses, the care of children while a parent is dying and after the death is a major burden for immediate and extended families. Increasingly, one hears that the extended family system is overwhelmed by the magnitude of the burden of caring for so many orphaned children. The

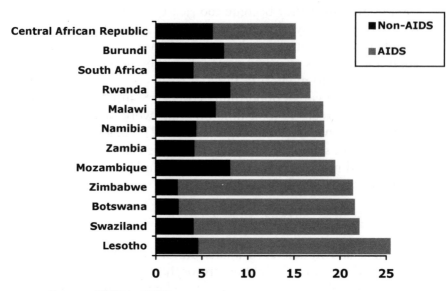

Source: CHGA, 2005
Figure 3.2 Estimated orphans in twelve countries of sub-Saharan Africa in 2010 as a percentage of all children

changes in living arrangements, well-being and opportunities for a secure future for children are among the most significant long-term outcomes of the HIV/AIDS pandemic. Although HIV/AIDS is but one cause of orphanhood, it plays an ever-increasing role in removing parents from their children. A sizeable portion of children in southern and eastern Africa are orphans. For example, one study found that almost a quarter (22 per cent) of all children under the age of 15 in the South Africa sample were maternal orphans in that they had lost either their mother or both parents. The greater number of these orphans are girls.

Children experience the stresses of parental illness. The emotional upheaval of seeing a dying parent may leave children feeling abandoned and increase their susceptibility to sexual abuse. A study in South Africa found that illness or death had resulted in 12 per cent of households sending children away to live elsewhere. Some children are encouraged by parents or foster parents to work to supplement household incomes. Others work out of economic necessity. An already bad situation is then exacerbated by the fact that many of these children wind up in the worst forms of child labour. Most working orphans surveyed in a study in Tanzania complained of a whole complex of problems, among them going without food, forced initiation to commercial sex work and failure to receive wages.

The International Labour Organization (ILO) has recently sponsored surveys in Tanzania, South Africa, Zambia and Zimbabwe that have confirmed the linkage between HIV/AIDS orphanhood and the likelihood that a child will work, frequently outside of the household and in conditions that are sexually and economically exploitative and prone to harassment or violence. Orphaned children in Zambia have been found to be twice as likely to be working as non-orphaned children. At home, once a household member became ill the children's participation in domestic and farm work increased, often interfering with schooling, and detrimental to their health. AIDS orphans were also found to shoulder a big portion of the household and farm chores in foster homes.

Although most children are cared for within some family arrangement, there are a significant and growing number who have lost both parents and live in child-headed households without an adult presence. It is estimated that nearly 7 per cent of Zambia's nearly two million households are without any adult member, and are headed by a boy or a girl aged 14 or younger (Schubert, 2003). Surveys found between 2 and 4 per cent of children in Gweru, Zimbabwe, lived in child-headed households (Zimbabwe National AIDS Council, 2004). A similar survey in Tanzania found that over 9 per cent of children lived alone, essentially heading a household – at least where a house and living arrangements actually existed (Semkiwa et al., 2003).

While they represent only a small proportion of all households, child-headed households and children living on the street without any adult supervision present an especially important challenge for policy makers, programme planners and service agencies alike. The existence of children living on their own is a new phenomenon in Africa and is a manifestation of social disruption and social inequalities associated with HIV/AIDS. Child-headed households exist because no relatives are left to care for the children, or else the surviving relatives are already too burdened to care adequately for the children they have inherited. Many children who become household heads have little option but to seek work to support themselves and their siblings. Stories exist of older children earning the cash to keep younger siblings in school; however, continued schooling for any of the children in these households is problematic.

As noted above, orphaned children, including children in households with a parent ill with HIV/AIDS or related illness, may find their education cut short and future economic opportunities compromised. Children from families where one or more adults are HIV-infected are more likely than children in non-affected households to be withdrawn from school because families cannot afford the school costs, need the children to help supplement household income, or need them to help care for sick relatives. These trends are especially evident in countries with high HIV/AIDS rates and where school fees and costs are relatively high for low-income groups. In Zambia, rural orphaned children have a 20 per cent higher rate of school non-attendance than non-orphaned children (Schubert, 2003). In western Kenya, 20 per cent of households with orphaned children report having no children in school, primarily because of lack of money (Odipo, 2000). Girls, more often than boys, are withdrawn from school or have entry postponed.

Changes in Extended Family Systems

One of the major issues arising from the impact of HIV/AIDS on households is the ability and willingness of extended family members to assist in the care of remaining family members, especially children who have been orphaned. As noted earlier, a prevailing assumption in many national HIV/AIDS policies is that 'traditional' family structures could and will cope with the pressures caused by the epidemic. A growing number of field studies bring that assumption into doubt. Particularly in light of major social and economic changes of the past several decades (and stretching back well into the colonial era), what is often referred to as the 'extended family' takes numerous forms across Africa and offers numerous variations on coping with the impact of HIV/AIDS. At the most simplistic, family members who have settled for two or three decades (or more) in urban centres may have weak links with their wider family. Social networks may actually have become stronger than family membership for some people. Families which have little contact with their extended family have greater likelihood of orphans being abandoned should the current caregiver die. While it is not an either/or situation (i.e. extended families are coping or they are not), it does appear that HIV/AIDS is inducing new pressures on many families that increasingly find it difficult to cope.

A good portion of the burden of support for affected families and family members falls to older adults. A study in rural Zimbabwe found that grandmothers were the primary caregivers for orphaned children or children left behind when one or both parents went to look for work (or land) elsewhere (WHO, 2002a). Another study in Zimbabwe found that half of all foster parents for orphaned children were grandparents and that over 60 per cent of fostering households were headed by women (SAFAIDS/CFU, 1996). A study in KwaZulu-Natal Province of South Africa found that 57 per cent of households caring for orphaned children were headed by women who, on average, were 59 years old – i.e. likely to be grandmothers (Hosegood et al., 2003). Yet a fourth study, from rural southern Zambia, found that nearly 70 per cent of all households caring for orphaned children were headed either by a woman of any age or by an elderly person (Rau, 2003).

In other cases, relatives with jobs are expected to play a larger role in direct support for extended family members (such as fostering a child) or indirect support (providing money for medical expenses or school fees). It is not unusual in eastern and southern Africa to find salaried workers supporting two, three or more extended family members with their earnings.

The Dissolution of Households

Under the impact of HIV/AIDS it appears that a significant number of households cease to exist, especially if the deceased is a woman. If both parents die, the children are likely to live with other relatives, or, as noted, care for themselves. Emerging data from the Commission on HIV/AIDS and governance in Africa (CHGA) research covering both rural and urban areas of Zimbabwe seem to indicate that 'sixty-five per cent of the households where the deceased adult female used to live before her death were reported to be no longer in existence' (CHGA, 2004a, p. 12). Other studies have found that deceased wives are more likely to be replaced – the widowed man remarries (Kaliyati et al., 2003). However, the children from the previous marriage may still be sent away, and so remarriage does not necessarily mean that the members of the original household stay together. Either migration or dissolution seems to follow the death of an HIV-infected responsible adult in a family, according to a study in rural KwaZulu-Natal Province, South Africa (Steinberg et al., 2002). There, households where an adult member has died of HIV/AIDS or related causes were nearly three times more likely to have dissolved by the end of the year than other households (Hosegood et al., 2003, p. 14).

The Impact of HIV/AIDS on Women and Girls

Women and girls face an inordinate burden in the era of HIV/AIDS. Not only are girls and young women at greater risk of HIV/AIDS than their male counterparts, the impact of household illnesses and deaths causes greater sacrifices by females. This is not to minimize the impact of HIV/AIDS on boys and men, but economic, social and cultural patterns place males in more favourable positions to cope with the impact. Existing gender inequalities intensify along with the pandemic. Women may have to give up jobs and income-earning to care for a sick spouse or relative. The burden of caregiving falls primarily on women, and that burden carries over into dealing with the possible loss of assets to relatives upon the death of a husband. Girls tend to be withdrawn from school earlier than or rather than boys, to assist with caregiving, household chores and family income support. There are widespread anecdotal reports of men seeking ever younger girls for sexual purposes, including those under 12 years of age, on the assumption that the girls are not HIV-infected or that the man will be cured of his infection.

Girls in households affected by HIV/AIDS are twice as likely as boys to have dropped out of school, because families could not pay the school fees or needed the children for household help (Badcock-Walters et al., 2003). In addition, girls and women are subject to sexual exploitation and abuse. A study in Kenya found that the most important reason for high infection rates among girls is the frequency of sexual intercourse with older men (Odipo, 2000). 'Sugar daddies', as they are known around the world, seduce naïve and impressionable girls with offers of cash, consumer goods and supposed status. In the war-like conditions of Burundi, the threat of forced sex is a weapon used by men against women and girls. In turn, women and girls may agree to sexual relationships in exchange for some level of physical and material security. Household violence towards women and girls is increasingly being documented and linked to HIV/AIDS transmission. Girls who have been orphaned by HIV/AIDS and who lack strong family support and peer networks may become vulnerable to further sexual harass-ment and exploitation. Lack of appropriate legal mechanisms to address such abuse creates conditions where this can continue. A report from Botswana argues that amongst children aged 5 to 15, sexual abuse by older males may well account for the majority of, if not all, new HIV/AIDS infections (IRIN, 2003).

This is part of the reason for the major disparities in HIV/AIDS infection rates between adolescent girls and boys. For example, in major urban areas of eastern and southern Africa, epidemiological studies have shown that 17 to 22 per cent of girls aged 15 to 19 are already HIV-infected compared with 3 to 7 per cent of boys of similar age (CHGA, 2003).

In addition to possibly becoming the head of a household, women face other burdens. A study in the early 1990s in areas of Uganda highly affected by HIV/AIDS noted the following potential situations faced by widows (Topouzis, 1994). The scenarios can be applied to many societies. Women may experience:

- the loss of land and perhaps the right to use the land;
- the loss of their property to the husband's family, unless the husband has left a will – women often do not inherit property when their husbands die;
- an enforced relationship with the late husband's brother or other male relative, rejection of which would result in them having to return to their maternal home;
- the assumption of sole responsibility for the children, with limited outside support;
- a significant loss of cash income;
- the loss of access to support services that traditionally go to men, such as agricultural services and the loss of farm production knowledge for work done by men; and
- an increased workload as they struggle to meet basic needs.

The report further notes that HIV/AIDS contributes to a dramatic rise of female-headed households through the death of a male spouse, and that in such households many AIDS widows are younger than previously has been the case, and therefore still have young children to care for. Most female-headed households tend to be among the poorest in communities across Africa. Again, HIV/AIDS is intensifying, if not deepening, the gender inequities of society.

In western Kenya, a study found that some households cope with the loss of an adult member by encouraging the marriage of a teenage daughter in order to gain the financial assets (i.e. cattle or other livestock) of a dowry (Kenyan Ministry of Health, 2002). The same study noted that in households in which a female spouse had died, children were likely to be sent to live with relatives or in other households. In contrast, the death of a non-spouse female adult is associated with an increase in the number of boys in the household. This is most likely to help out with household activities formerly handled by the now-deceased female adult. This indicates, as might be expected, that the effects of adult death do not depend only on the age and gender of the deceased, but also on the position of the individual in the household.

Impacts on Rural Livelihoods

Most people in sub-Saharan African continue to live in, or have strong connections to, rural areas. Agriculture continues to be the primary source of home food consumption and income for those people. While the HIV/AIDS epidemics have tended to be more concentrated in urban, peri-urban and local market areas, by 2005 few rural communities had been spared the impacts of the disease. The agricultural base of rural societies – and most African nations – is affected, as are the livelihoods of many rural people. Already weak rural services have become more tenuous and there is an increase in rural poverty. People already impoverished face even more desperate situations as HIV/AIDS saps their limited labour supplies and assets.

In summarizing its research on the impact of HIV/AIDS on land and production in eastern and southern Africa, the Food and Agriculture Organization of the United Nations

(FAO) concludes: '. . . HIV/AIDS will seriously impact on a range of land issues and livelihood strategies. These issues include different forms of land use, various types of land tenure and land reform projects that are most appropriate, the functioning of land administration systems, the land rights of women and orphans as well of the poor generally, and inheritance practices and norms' (Tumushabe, 2003). In the fifteen years between 1985 and 2000, the FAO estimated that globally 7 million agricultural workers had died due to HIV/AIDS. That number has increased substantially since 2000. It is important to note that the impacts of HIV/AIDS on rural societies are not uniform, a point to which we shall return.

HIV/AIDS affects rural livelihoods at several levels. It means a loss of labour for food and income production. People are too weak to work or are caring for family members who are ill. A survey in rural Zambia found that heads of households who were chronically ill reduced the area of land they cultivated by half, resulting in reduced crop production and lower food availability (Waller, 1998). In rural Zimbabwe, maize output by households that experienced a death due to AIDS declined by nearly half (see table 3.3). The government of Swaziland reported a 54 per cent drop in agricultural production in AIDS-affected households (Swaziland, 2002). Lowered production due to the loss of

Table 3.3 Reduction of output in a household with an AIDS death, Zimbabwe

Crop	Reduction in output (%)
Maize	61
Cotton	47
Vegetables	49
Groundnuts	37
Cattle	29

Source: Kwaramba, 1997

household labour often carries over for one or more years after a death occurs. Some households, especially those already short on household labour, may never recover to levels of previous production.

Even before a person dies of AIDS, illness curtails the work that can be done and the income earned. Case studies in Tanzania and Zambia have estimated that households lose around two years of labour by the time of death of an adult. Lowered production and time for off-farm work leave households with a chronically ill member with, on average, reductions in annual income of 30 to 35 per cent (Mutangadura and Webb 1999; Rugalema, 1998). In two villages in Burkina Faso revenues from agricultural production declined by 25 to 50 per cent because of AIDS. After an adult death, funeral expenses further reduce household income (UNDP, 2001).

Urban residents who are ill with AIDS often return to their rural homes in their final months or weeks of life. About 20 to 30 per cent of those living in one division of Nyeri, Kenya, who were HIV positive returned to their rural homesteads when they could no longer work. 'This has further increased the burden on rural households with scant financial resources' (Drimie 2002, p. 14; see also Ainsworth and Semali, 1995). Caregiving, predominately a role for women and girls, results in less time spent on care of livestock, crop production and other income-generating activities.

During these periods of chronic illness related to HIV/AIDS, households disinvest – that is, they spend down their saving and sell assets to compensate for lost income and new expenses. In cattle-owning communities, animals are frequently sold to meet costs. For example, in pastoral communities in Uganda, over 13 per cent of the households that had cattle had sold off animals 'to meet family needs resulting from HIV/AIDS'. In mixed farming households, nearly one-third (32 per cent) reportedly had sold animals to pay for medical care and other household expenses (Topouzis, 1994). In Namibia livestock and grain sales are common ways to raise money to meet illness-related expenses or to replace lost income. In widow-headed households, distress sales and the dispossession of property are increasing to cope with the loss of adult male labour and income (Engh et al., 2000). A study in western Kenya confirmed the trends. In disinvestments of assets by households experiencing a prime-age adult death, sales of small livestock would occur before those of cattle. The authors note that some households with a prime-age adult death could even gain cattle through dowry, as daughters were married off as a way to gain new assets (Yamano and Jayne, 2002). Rugalema (as quoted in Topouzis, 2000) reports that thirty-nine of the fifty-two AIDS-afflicted households in a Tanzanian village had sold one or more assets in direct response to AIDS morbidity. Nearly a quarter (24 per cent) of Zimbabwean households affected by an adult female death sold assets to cope with the death (Mutangadura, 2000). In Swaziland, AIDS-related deaths have specific impacts on crop yield, remittances and size of area under cultivation compared to non-AIDS deaths (see figure 3.3).

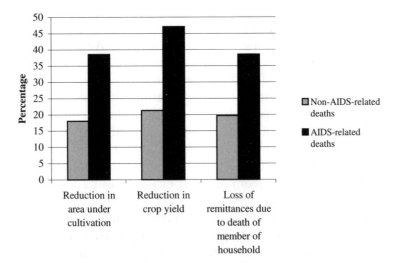

Source: FAO Committee on World Food Security, 2001
Figure 3.3 Impact of AIDS-related death on crop production and household incomes, Swaziland

The labour and financial pressures imposed by HIV/AIDS on the agricultural production of households often results in a shift in production from cash to food crops. A 2002 survey in Malawi found that most households with a chronically ill adult shifted their crop mix to less labour-intense crops (CHGA, 2004a). In Uganda and Namibia, studies have shown households giving less attention to livestock, with the result that animals had died 'due to poor management or [were] stolen after the death of able-bodied household members' (Ugandan Ministry of Agriculture, Animal Industry and Fisheries, 2002, p. 16; see also Engh et al., 2000). Larger or wealthier households were able to hire labour to assist with agricultural tasks, but that was not the case with low-income households, especially those headed by women.

As adults die, the acquired knowledge of farming practices may be lost. Family members who have to assume new or greater responsibilities for farming often do so without an adequate understanding of livestock care, soil and plant types, or land preparation methods. A family's social and support networks may also suffer, as less time is devoted to community formal and informal activities.

The Economic Impact on Households and Communities

HIV/AIDS is costly to most households and communities (see table 3.1). During periods of illness, medical costs rise, work and incomes are disrupted, family members are drawn away from work to provide care, and in some instances children have to work to supplement household incomes. After death, funerals can be expensive, sometimes costing more than the amount previously spent on medical care. The loss of an adult undermines a family's income-generating abilities, adding to the work burden of surviving family members, including children. AIDS-affected families may experience rapid transition from relative wealth to relative poverty. For poorer and rural households, the ability to cope with external shocks, such as drought or increases in the prices of staple products, will be reduced further.

What stands out from numerous studies over the past decade is how HIV/AIDS induces impoverishment of many households (though not all, and how many in a particular community or region is unclear). Income is lost and assets are sold or rented in order to get cash. There appears to be widespread disinvestment of assets as households spend their savings and wealth to cope with HIV/AIDS. This section sets out some of the economic conditions that follow the disease.

Loss of Income

The economic impact of HIV/AIDS is significant and often dramatic in terms of changes in income, asset wealth and longer-term prospects for economic security. A study in KwaZulu-Natal, South Africa, found that households that had experienced a death in the previous twelve months (not only from HIV/AIDS, it needs to be pointed out) had a mean monthly income equal to only 64 per cent of households that had not experienced a death (Cogneau and Grimm, 2002). Another South African study in the Free State Province found that HIV/AIDS-affected households tended to have monthly incomes one-third less than non-affected households (Booysen and Bachmann, 2002). In the Côte d'Ivoire, the income of affected families was half that of total average household income (Béchu, 1998).

The burden of caregiving can deepen the poverty of households, moving some of them into destitution. A household study in southern Zambia found households with very high dependency ratios of three to five times national averages, primarily, but not exclusively, due to the caring burdens created by HIV/AIDS (UNICEF, 1998). In these households, labour that might contribute to household necessities or income simply did not exist. Children in these households are likely to have to work in order to survive.

Efforts are made to draw on resources from wherever possible, utilizing existing family and social networks. A study based on household data in Rakai, Uganda, one of the earliest centres of the HIV/AIDS epidemic, showed that extended family members, community members and NGOs provided from 40 to nearly 70 per cent of the medical and burial costs experienced by affected families (Konde-Lule et al., 1993).

Shifts in Spending

The burden of medical and related expenses induces changes in family spending patterns. In Côte d'Ivoire in the mid-1990s, households affected by HIV/AIDS spent nearly twice the proportion of their budgets on medical care compared to those that were not affected (Béchu, 1998). In Rwanda, a household survey found expenses on health care to be over twenty times higher in HIV/AIDS-affected, as compared to non-affected, households (Nandakumar et al., 2000). Further, health care expenses for men were 2.6 times greater than for women, illustrating deep biases in accessing and using health care. Expenditures at this level became a major burden on family budgets. Among households affected by HIV/AIDS in the Kagera region of Tanzania, almost all cash income was used to pay medical bills relating to HIV/AIDS (Tibaijuka, 1997).

As medical expenses climb, spending on other items tends to decline. In South Africa, households with an AIDS-sick member were found to reduce spending on necessities. The most likely expenses to be cut were clothing (21 per cent), electricity (16 per cent) and other services (9 per cent). Some 6 per cent of affected families reduced spending on food (Booysen and Bachmann, 2002). While not as high a percentage as might be expected, most families reported that they already had insufficient food at various times. Spending on food and education may be reduced significantly, as in Côte d'Ivoire, where spending on basic consumption items (food and accommodation) fell by 40 per cent after the death of a family member from AIDS. These cuts in basic necessities further contribute to overall household poverty as malnutrition, health of children and women, and future work opportunities are compromised.

The 'savings' incurred through these cuts in spending on necessities were used for medical care and drugs for the person living with HIV/AIDS. The spending on health care was far higher in rural than urban locations, and in both cases was six to twelve times greater than the national average. Withdrawing children from school or delaying their entry is another way in which some families adjust spending patterns.

Paying for the Costs of HIV/AIDS

Households meet the costs of HIV/AIDS in a variety of ways, in addition to changing spending patterns. New members may be added to the household to compensate for a lost adult member. Loans may be acquired from relatives or neighbours. Assets may be sold, including, as noted above, grain, cattle and other livestock. A study from the Rakai region in Uganda found that only those households that experienced a death due to HIV/AIDS (as opposed to a death due to other causes) had a depletion in resources (Topouzis, 1994). Health care and funeral expenses related to HIV/AIDS, coupled with loss of income, therefore lead to rapid depletion of household resources.

In one study in Zimbabwe, 24 per cent of surveyed households sold an asset to cope with the death of the adult female (WHO, 2002a). There was a greater chance that assets would be sold among rural than among urban households. Cattle and smaller livestock, clothing and household furniture were the items more commonly sold. Disinvestment can continue after the death of a male adult in the household. In the Oshana region of Namibia, it was found that in households where the husband died of HIV/AIDS, livestock, sometimes all animals, are taken by relatives from the surviving family members (Engh et al., 2000).

As noted above, funeral expenses can add significantly to the economic burden of households and communities experiencing HIV/AIDS. One South African survey found that, on average, funeral costs were equivalent to one-third of annual household income (Desmond and Gow, 2001). In another study, this in KwaZulu-Natal, South Africa, funeral costs represented the equivalent of two months' mean household income (Badcock-Walters et al., 2003).

In the months and years after a death, the ability to earn income is reduced and surviving households may sell additional assets, borrow or search for new sources of income. In a household study in Free State Province, South Africa, HIV/AIDS-affected families (already poorer than non-affected families) tended to borrow first and then sell assets (Hosegood et al., 2003). In that study, affected households largely spent the borrowed money on medical expenses and funerals, while non-affected households generally used the money for education, durables and clothing. The same study also found that HIV/AIDS impacts on savings disproportionately. Affected households on average utilized twenty-one months' worth of savings, while non-affected households only utilized five months' worth of current savings.

Differentiation in Coping with the Costs of HIV/AIDS

The ability to deal with the economic pressures arising from HIV/AIDS varies according to the wealth, size and social position of households. Findings from a rural area of eastern Zimbabwe indicated that 'the key differentiating factor between HIV/AIDS-affected households and others within a particular category is that their capacity to cope with any shock is severely compromised by not having additional labour of their own to rely on' (Save the Children UK, 2002). Thus, the size of a household, the person who is ill/dies, the level of household assets and the ability (with cash, kind or social arrangement) to call in additional labour play a pivotal role in managing an AIDS-related death and the time it takes to adjust to the loss.

As might be expected, poorer households respond differently from better-off households. Analysis of data generated in the Kagera region of Tanzania found that among the poorer half of households, both food expenditure and food consumption fall dramatically in the six months following a death of an adult member of a household, in contrast to increases in non-poor households suffering a death (Lundberg et al., 2000). The differences are not simply a reflection of relative wealth, but of decisions about how to cope with an adult death. One method used more by wealthier than poorer people is acquiring informal forms of credit and transfers. Such forms of 'informal insurance' are available only to a limited extent to the poorest households; however, the latter may get some assistance from formal structures, such as the government.

Findings from a rural area of eastern Zimbabwe indicated that the capacity of HIV/AIDS-affected households to cope with shock is severely compromised by not having additional labour of their own to rely on, as opposed to non-affected households (Wilkins, 2003). Thus, the size of a household, the person who is ill/dies, the level of household assets and the ability (with cash, kind or social arrangement) to call in additional labour play a pivotal role in managing an AIDS-related death and the time it takes to adjust to the loss.

The death of an adult male is especially costly in terms of lost income and assets. By contrast, when the wife dies, livestock assets and grain production are less affected, in part because fewer resources are invested in the medical care of women. Grain production levels are usually maintained, although tasks normally done by women, such as weeding, may decline in intensity. However, when a male head dies, high-value or cash crop production changes, as the available household labour is devoted to food crops.

In Uganda, one study showed that 44 per cent of respondents reported reduced variety of crops in the last ten years, in response to reductions in labour supply due to AIDS (FAO Committee on World Food Security, 2001). Reduction was more common in female-headed households (77.3 per cent), especially those where the woman was widowed. In Zimbabwe, food consumption in households where a woman had died declined and variety narrowed (Mutangadura, 2000). It should be noted, however, that it is difficult to distinguish between changes in food consumption arising from the death of a woman and those resulting from the economic hardships of a contracting economy.

Of course, where households are already poor or very poor, there is little to sell. Outside assistance by religious and community groups and family and friends played a large role in helping HIV/AIDS-affected households in Rwanda to meet the financial burdens arising from the epidemic. In that country, two-thirds of surveyed households were found to receive some kind of assistance. Eighteen per cent had to borrow money to pay for care, and 5 per cent had to sell assets (Nandakumar et al., 2000). In Zimbabwe, following an adult female death, a study found that female-headed households relied more heavily on remittance from family members, informal activities and agriculture and subletting. Male-headed households, on the other hand, depended more on the use of savings, followed by borrowing from informal sources and remittances from family members.

The Widening and Deepening of Poverty

The pattern of coping, outlined for poor and very poor urban households in Burundi, illustrates how the circumstances arising from the impact of HIV/AIDS intensify poverty (Niyongabo, 2001):

- the expectation of child labour, at an increasingly young age;
- decreased/interrupted payments for basic services (school);
- interrupted debt reimbursements;
- increased demands to the community for gifts in cash or kind;
- sale of sex, for cash or in-kind payments;
- begging;

- sale of household goods; and
- shared housing, with three to four women plus children sharing one room.

Clearly, the struggle of poor households to deal with the multiple losses arising from HIV/AIDS is pushing members into increasingly desperate and risky situations. For these households, the basic goal is to survive and on a daily basis find ways to manage with minimal resources. Existing poverty is exacerbated by HIV/AIDS and is contributing to destitution.

Larger and better-endowed households are less likely than smaller households to become poor as a result of HIV/AIDS. They are better able to distribute the impacts of medical care and funeral expenses, as well as loss of labour and income, across family members and through social networks. Simulation modelling in Botswana indicates a fall of 18 per cent by 2010 in the average income of households in the lowest quartile. This is nearly double the income loss in the population as a whole (Greener, 2000). Similarly, modelling of the pandemic in Burkina Faso predicted that with a stabilized HIV prevalence rate of 10 per cent in 2005, the incidence of poverty would increase from 45 to 53 per cent after fourteen years (from 1997 through to 2010) (UNDP, 2001).

The intuitive implication of these findings is that HIV/AIDS intensifies prevailing income inequalities in society. However, the Botswana simulation does not predict any change in the level of income inequality. This is explained by an overall downward shift in per capita incomes. In other words, societies as a whole are becoming poorer as a result of HIV/AIDS. Three observations, however, arise from the findings of the Botswana simulation:

- Inequalities are already significant in Botswana. HIV/ AIDS sustains those patterns during the overall downward shift in poverty levels across society.
- The models do not adequately take into account the most impoverished, the households that become destitute or dissolve altogether.

• Access to services, a factor of poverty and inequality, is not included in the equations.

For Botswana, and other countries with advanced epidemics, the pandemic narrows the range of opportunities for reducing economic and social inequalities while deepening national poverty. As noted earlier, access to education is already compromised for many children affected by HIV/AIDS. In the health sector, access to affordable treatment and adequate health services has become one of the most important differentiating factors in HIV-related survival between rich and poor countries and communities.

In summary, the economic impact of HIV/AIDS on households and communities is far-reaching and is likely to worsen over the coming decade. In the absence of significant subsidies for medical and drug care, households will be spending a significant portion of their incomes on health care. To pay for health care, assets will be sold, further impoverishing many households. Extended family and community members will face increasing demands on their resources to assist affected households. Some households will be better able to cope with these changes and will recover economic stability after several months or years. Others, however, will become economically worse off. Poverty will intensify. What proportion of all affected households will be most adversely impacted remains speculative, but given the prevalence of poverty in many African countries, it is reasonable to suggest that at least half of HIV/AIDS-affected households will experience long-term economic distress.

With national services and community and household resources already strained, it is difficult to foresee quick fixes that will alleviate the economic and social impacts of HIV/AIDS. Rather, a development-based orientation is needed. Elements of a development response will include large-scale job creation and youth job training, infrastructure rebuilding and substantial subsidies for local development initiatives. Whether it is through targeted initiatives or broad, national-scale programmes, development efforts must be

designed and implemented that minimize the impoverishment and inequalities that are occurring in the wake of the
HIV/AIDS epidemic.

Macro-economic Impacts and Implications

There is no quantifiable threshold at which the social impact
of the epidemic becomes visible, but some evidence that
the impact is not immediate can be obtained from life
expectancy. Life expectancy is an indicator that is widely
used in econometric regressions because it is found to be significantly correlated with various economic and health vari-
ables. It therefore makes sense to ask the question of how
high the HIV prevalence rate has to be for life expectancy
to decline. The answer is shown by figure 3.4, which plots
the change in life expectancy in the 1990s for developing
countries against the 1999 HIV prevalence rate among
adults. This graph indicates that life expectancy increased for
all countries where the adult HIV prevalence rate was less
than 5 per cent, but declined once the HIV prevalence rate

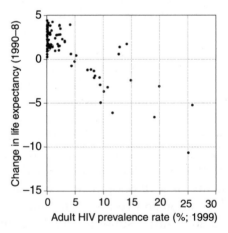

Figure 3.4 HIV prevalence and life expectancy (ninety-four developing countries)

reached 5 per cent. To a large extent the 5 per cent threshold appears arbitrary. But what is important is that it highlights the lag between: the beginning of the HIV infection; the moment when it becomes an epidemic (around a prevalence rate of 2 per cent); and the time it starts to have a visible demographic impact. And it is only afterwards that the economic impact starts to appear.

As noted at the start of this chapter, it is this slow-acting nature of the HIV/AIDS epidemic that makes it so destructive compared to other diseases, for by the time it has become 'visible', it is usually too late to avoid its economic and developmental damage.

From the current literature we know that HIV/AIDS affects socio-economic development, through a number of channels, at macro and micro levels. Development is undercut through the loss of human capacity, the deteriorating performance of key organizations (revenue departments, central banks, legal authorities and ministries of education and health) and the fragmentation of vital economic networks. These have a non-linear, incremental impact on economic growth – the longer they persist, the more difficult/costly recovery becomes. Evidence of this has been most apparent in southern Africa over recent years in the wake of shocks such as famine, floods, fluctuating external commodity prices, regional disturbances and transport difficulties.

Over the past decade a number of studies have used quantitative estimates to model how these multiple effects are likely to impact on the long-term economic growth of the most severely affected African states. Over (1992) estimated that between 1990 and 2025 the ten countries with the most advanced epidemics would see a reduction in growth per capita of a third of a percentage point compared to a non-AIDS scenario. Similarly, Cuddington and Hancock (1994) suggest that between 1985 and 2010 Malawi could experience average real GDP growth up to 1.5 percentage points lower, while Cuddington (1993) estimates that in Tanzania per capita GDP could be up to 10 per cent smaller. A 2000 application of the model by the Botswana Institute for

Development Analysis estimated that the GDP growth rate in Botswana would be reduced by 1.5 per cent and that over thirty-five years the total effect would be an economy 25 per cent smaller than otherwise (Greener, 2000) (table 3.4).

A more sophisticated recent World Bank study of South Africa suggests that the economy could shrink by a third by 2078 because of HIV/AIDS (Bell et al., 2003). The interesting thing to note about this study is that it used a new-generation model incorporating a broader range of retrogressive effects than earlier models. Specifically, it allowed for reductions in human capital, declining savings and investment rates, disintegrating households, increasing poverty, falling labour productivity and impaired institutions.

The value of any projection, of course, depends on how realistic the underlying assumptions are regarding the various trends. It is here that the lack of appropriate data becomes important, not least because it completely distorts the true picture. Take the case of the World Bank Study of South Africa, where the HIV prevalence rate exceeds 20 per cent. Although the cumulative loss implies a reduction in growth of GDP by 2080 of roughly a third, in per annum terms it translates to between only 0.4 and 0.9 per cent. This is not a trivial change, but it could easily be produced by other factors that also affect growth – revenue shocks, falling commodity prices, drought and civil unrest – to mention but a few. Seen in this light, estimates from a wide range of countries also reveal that none of the projected effects of HIV/AIDS on economic growth is large; certainly not enough to compel governments with a limited political life span into immediate action.

The problem lies at the high level of abstraction. The advantage of GDP is that it is an effective indicator of macro movements as it relies almost exclusively on aggregate data. Unfortunately the HIV/AIDS pandemic is unfolding at the micro level – with significant psycho-social impacts on family members, particularly children, that are difficult to capture in aggregate terms. Moreover, the majority of HIV infections at any one time are asymptomatic and the full effects of the

Table 3.4 Comparison of macro-economic studies

	Predicted impact	Author	Forecast period
Africa (thirty countries)	GDP growth rate falls by 0.6 to 1.5%	Over (1992)	1990–2025
Cameroon	GDP growth rate falls by 0.5 to 1.2%	Kambou et al. (1992)	
Tanzania	GDP growth falls from 3.9% without AIDS to 2.8–3.3%	Cuddington (1993)	1985–2010
Malawi	GDP growth rate is reduced by 0.2 to 1.5%	Cuddington and Hancock (1994)	1985–2010
Botswana	GDP growth rate falls from 3.9% to 2–3.1%	Botswana Institute for Development Policy Analysis (BIDPA) (2000)	1996–2001
Mozambique	GDP growth rate falls	Arndt (2002)	1999–2010
Developing countries (80)	Per capita growth rate falls by 0.8% for sub-Saharan African countries	Bonnel (2000)	1990–7
South Africa	By 2010 GDP is 17% smaller than it would be otherwise	Arndt and Lewis (2000)	1997–2010

HIV epidemic on mortality and orphanhood take decades to unfold. These factors are central to understanding the difficulties of mapping the long-term development implications of the pandemic. The time delay compromises the ability of analysts to monitor and fully capture the true nature of the threat that it poses. In turn, this also acts to slow down the nature of response needed to effectively safeguard societies and communities against the effects of the pandemic – thus delaying the rewards of action.

Despite the rather modest aggregate impacts being recorded by current studies, rational economic logic suggests that larger economic losses will occur and that African countries will find it increasingly difficult for their economies and societies to recover. While this might not be immediately clear at the level of aggregates (i.e. GDP), reductions in labour supply due to declining life expectancy will eventually adversely affect output; an impact that will be compounded by reduction in productive efficiency associated with increased incidences of ill health and shortages of critical skills. In addition, such decline in economic activity will take place against a background of rising social service expenditure, both private and public, which will strain government budgets and is likely to reduce savings rates as well as to increase poverty.

There will also be a range of indirect effects arising from the aggregate economic impacts and the increase in poverty. These can be expected to reduce the ability of governments to raise tax revenues (since these depend on the size of the economy), while increasing the demands on government expenditure, including poverty alleviation measures. Although there may be some saving arising from reduced population growth, we would expect HIV/AIDS to exacerbate the pressures for deficit spending by government, including dependence on overseas development assistance. It will also distort development spending on other areas, since it will be necessary to use valuable resources in 'defensive' or socially unproductive ways.

A cross-country econometric analysis of growth among eighty developing countries conducted by René Bonnel (2000) illustrates the position perfectly. On average the per capita income of African countries was found to grow by 0.8 percentage points per year fewer than otherwise. While small in magnitude, the effects become quite large over time. For the high HIV prevalence countries, the economic cost of HIV/AIDS is staggering. In the case of a typical sub-Saharan country with a prevalence rate of 20 per cent, GDP would be 67 per cent less than otherwise at the end of a twenty-year period. One reason for the large impact of HIV/AIDS is that it also provides an opportunity for other diseases such as tuberculosis to thrive.

One implication of the above results is that highly infected countries would sink into poverty. But, as mentioned before, the economic impact of HIV/AIDS depends greatly on the initial status of development of countries. There may be a threshold that determines whether countries will either continue to grow (although at a slower rate) or sink into stagnation or economic decline. For countries where the HIV/AIDS prevalence rate is quite high, the loss of labour and human capital may be so great that per capita income falls to a level such that households can no longer save enough for the stock of capital to increase. As a result, these countries would experience sustained economic decline over the long term unless the source of the decline was addressed and international assistance was mobilized to finance effective HIV/AIDS interventions.

The impact on households with HIV normally follows the same pattern: loss of income, if a breadwinner stops work due to sickness or death (this is a permanent impact); loss of income if a breadwinner has to stop work to look after a sick family member (this is a temporary or transient impact); and additional expenditure on health care and eventually funeral costs (a transient impact). An AIDS death brings with it loss of productive resources through the sale of livestock to pay for sickness, mourning and funeral expenses, as well as sharp decline in productivity. Sickness also contributes to the scarcity of labour because of both the incapacity of workers and the time others have to devote to looking after them. The net effect of these losses is that such households rarely recover even their initial level of living, since their capacity is eroded. As a result, a true process of structural economic decline quickly sets in. It is therefore reasonable to expect that HIV/AIDS will give rise to an increase in the proportion of poor households.

In contrast, countries that are initially well endowed with human and physical capital may not experience a substantial increase in poverty over time. What determines the outcome is the size of the HIV/AIDS 'shock'. If the initial shock is small, it is quite likely that the growth process will continue, although at a lower rate. But if the shock is large, growth may be interrupted and replaced by economic decline. This outcome could occur if, for example, the HIV/AIDS epidemic was allowed to spread for an extended period of time.

Concluding Remarks

It appears that only a small percentage of affected households benefit from state social welfare and support programmes to mitigate the impact of HIV/AIDS or to reach very poor families. In Zimbabwe, it was reported that no more than 2 per cent of people in need receive such support. A South African state grant programme for older adults does provide some minimal financial assistance, but usually not enough for grandparents to adequately care for fostered children. The state also offers grants for children, but not all parents/guardians are able to produce the required birth certificate to register for the grant. As of early 2000, less than 5 per cent of eligible children were benefiting from the monthly grants to guardians. In Zambia, the Ministry of Labour and Social Security offers grants to implementing NGOs for street children projects. Education reforms that have recently occurred in many countries are designed to offer free or reduced-fee education at primary school levels. These changes do offer some mitigation support to families, although many observers note that other costs for school attendance remain.

It is clear that across Africa, governments are not prepared and are budgetarily constrained in terms of offering financial support to individuals, families and communities affected by HIV/AIDS. In fact, most governments with HIV/AIDS policies and programmes stress that care and support will fall primarily on families; little mention is made of mitigation as a role of government. There is a growing willingness on the part of state governments to absorb some of the cost of providing antiretroviral drugs for pregnant women and newborn infants. In addition, some governments are paying for (or preparing to pay for) the cost of antiretroviral drugs for a select group of people living with HIV/AIDS. To date, however, only Botswana has implemented its programme to cover the costs of providing antiretroviral drugs to its citizens. As of mid-2003, some 9,000 people, in four priority groups, are receiving antiretroviral drugs in Botswana (Darkoh, 2005).

Broad social welfare, social transfer and job creation schemes exist on paper in numerous countries, but have been undermined by prevailing economic conditions and practices over the past two decades. In one district in southern Zambia, half of one per cent of potentially eligible people receive state welfare assistance, for example. In most African countries, pensions and other old age funds exist primarily for permanent public service employees. Likewise, many governments pay funeral and some medical costs for civil servants, thus reducing some financial pressures on affected households. Civil servant beneficiaries are likely, also, to receive a death benefit or have access to pension benefits. However, civil servants represent only a small portion of all adults in most countries.

National policies offer frameworks for developing interventions and guidance for other sectors in setting priorities and designing actions. Most countries in Africa now have HIV/AIDS policies and structures designed to co-ordinate policy development and programme implementation. There are, however, wide differences between countries (and also within some countries) in the effectiveness of multi-sectoral co-ordination. Malawi, for example, has on paper a structure that includes village AIDS committees that will facilitate local mobilization and activities. However, the local committees have not, for the most part, been activated or supported by either communities or outside agencies.

The national policies of most countries include statements about community responsibilities. These tend to stress the importance of home-based care for HIV-infected individuals and care for orphaned children by the extended family and communities. In 1994, Malawi became the first country in the region to develop a policy statement and guidelines on the care of orphans. The guidelines emphasize community-based responses, but the inability of communities to cope with the demands of the growing number of orphaned children prevents full and effective implementation of those community initiatives.

Several countries have policies, or drafts of policies, on child welfare. Most countries have signed ILO conventions that define a minimum age for work by children and prohibit children from working in especially harsh and risky occupations. All African countries have signed the Convention on the Rights of the Child, and many have signed up to regional conventions such as the African Charter on the Rights and Welfare of the Child. The ability of government authorities fully to enforce these and related international conventions is incomplete, however, especially given the stresses of poverty and the social and economic impact of HIV/AIDS on households. In most countries, obtaining the commitment of senior national political leaders to actual programme implementation is difficult. Moreover, existing programmes and organizations addressing the needs of orphans and vulnerable children are too small to organize lobbying at the required level.

The broad generalizations often drawn from the available evidence about the impact of HIV/AIDS, including the generalizations made in this chapter, require further testing and specification. Even the most commonly accepted assumptions about the impact of HIV/AIDS, such as the inability or unwillingness of extended families and communities to cope, need to be tested. It is not that the generalizations and assumptions are wrong. In many instances they are most likely correct, especially where evidence exists to confirm the statements. Rather, conditions of affected families and communities differ by a number of factors: socio-economic well-being prior to HIV/AIDS; size and demographic factors of households; prevailing social networks; local leadership; links to outside facilitating organizations and services. The inter-linkages between and the implications of these factors merit further investigation.

4
The Challenge of Scaling Up HIV/AIDS Treatment Programmes in Africa

Introduction

The issue of how best to move forward with comprehensive policies and programmes that aim to mitigate the social and economic impact of the HIV/AIDS pandemic has become a central concern for African policy makers. It is now increasingly clear that to achieve this objective, it is essential to address the issues of care and support for those affected, and to increase the access of PLWHA to effective treatment. Treatment should thus be seen as integral to policies and programmes that mitigate the impact of the epidemic on sustainable development. Indeed it is clear from a review of progress so far in implementing programmes for antiretroviral therapy (ART) that these activities are dependent on the collaboration and involvement of a wide range of partners drawn from the private and public sectors and from civil society.

Yet, many challenges stay in the way of scaling up AIDS treatment and care programmes in Africa. Among these are challenges related to the limited capacity of health systems, such as the low and declining number of health professionals, high drug prices, long-term financial sustainability, inadequate laboratory and patient care infrastructure, poor patient follow-up and poor sustainability of drug supply. Relatedly, scaling up treatment also requires fostering well-co-ordinated stakeholder buy-in on all fronts – involvement by the private sector, NGOs, faith-based organizations (FBOs) and communities – as well as ensuring equitable access to treatment and care and overcoming fear and stigma.

The aim of this chapter is three-fold: first, to make the case for the socio-economic and -political benefits of treating PLWHA in Africa; second, to conceptualize the scope and intensity of recent opportunities for AIDS treatment and care in Africa; third, to highlight some of the major challenges faced by African governments in scaling up programmes for treating and caring for people living with HIV/AIDS; and, finally, to identify some of the strategies needed to implement and sustain effective programmes across Africa. It is, however, with a brief overview of the challenged posed by HIV/AIDS to the continent's health system that I begin the analysis.

The Impact of HIV/AIDS on the Health Sector

In line with the analysis of the health implications of SAPs, today it is true to say that the programmes have had a tremendous impact over the past two decades. Whether rural health centres or urban public hospitals, many health facilities suffer from a shortage of qualified personnel, equipment and supplies. Patient care is affected. The morale of existing staff suffers as they try to cope with the heavy demands on their services. A rural district hospital in South Africa's KwaZulu-Natal Province – an area with some of the highest HIV rates in the country – experienced a 10 per cent increase in staff in the last half of the 1990s. Despite that improvement, staff were unable to deal with the increased patient load. Over half the nurses expressed dissatisfaction with their jobs and nearly 90 per cent reported being overworked. All reported being unable to offer quality care to patients, as they had been trained to do. Absenteeism among nurses and other staff increased three-fold over the period, adding pressure to the workload of others and adversely affecting the well-being of patients (Unger et al., 2002).

HIV/AIDS is crowding out services for other diseases, financially and in human terms. Part of the increased workload in health facilities is due to HIV/AIDS. A growing number of people seek medical care for AIDS and AIDS-related illnesses. A ten-year study of admissions to Kenyatta National Hospital in Nairobi showed that the rising numbers of AIDS patients displaced others in need of care from the hospital (Gilks, 1998). A study in South Africa found that HIV positive patients were, on average, hospitalized for twenty days while patients admitted for other ailments stayed an average of five days (Cullinan, 2003; Gauteng Health Department in South Africa, 2002). Another study, from Rwanda, found that HIV positive patients used health services at least twenty times more extensively than did non-HIV/AIDS patients. Further, men used the health services more than women. People living with HIV/AIDS in urban areas made over ten times the number of visits compared to those in rural areas, 'reflecting probably both the lack of access as well as the inability to pay' of rural people (Nandakumar et al., 2000). Numerous qualitative reports from across Africa support these findings.

Health care workers themselves are being lost to HIV/AIDS. Most studies indicate that public sector employees, including health workers, have HIV infection rates similar to the general population. A study in South Africa found over 16 per cent of health workers living with HIV/AIDS, with higher rates in some provinces and among younger and non-professional staff. Based on these data, the study reported that the country could lose up to 6,000 health workers per year to HIV/AIDS (Cullinan, 2003). Malawi's health services saw a three-fold increase in staff deaths between 1992 and 2000, with the greatest losses occurring in the age group between 30 and 44 (Malawi Institute of Management, 2002) (see table 4.1). HIV/AIDS places inordinate demands on public health facilities. On the one hand,

Table 4.1 Changes in established and vacant posts in the Malawi health sector

Staff category	Authorized establishment			% of established positions not filled		
	1992	1998[a]	2000	1992	1998	2000
Medical Officer	133	114	113	49	36	25
Clinical Officer	232	274	279	38	27	–
Medical Assistant	567	641	647	28	37	–
Registered Nurse	736	719	717	32	47	–
Enrolled Nurse Midwife	1,308	1,583	1,549	22	18	–
Environment Health Officer	27	130	114	15	27	–
Health Assistant	261	283	213	9	6	4
Health Surveillance Assistant	0	2,563	4,909	n/a	44	–
Laboratory Technician	31	33	33	42	33	–
Laboratory Assistant	18	107	109	33	28	50
Pharmacy Assistant	33	–	83	24	–	22

[a] Extrapolated and estimated from existing data (Malawi Institute of Management, from 2002).

public facilities are losing staff to the private sector. On the other hand, the drain on family finances from HIV/AIDS leads many to seek care, especially late in the progress of the disease, in lower-cost public facilities.

Despite the work of dedicated staff and the resources put into health care systems in sub-Saharan African countries, HIV/AIDS has intensified pressures on those systems. There are both more patients and more complicated conditions. Illnesses once thought to be under some control, such as tuberculosis, are re-surfacing and present new challenges to the medical establishment and communities. TB is closely associated with the declining immune system caused by HIV. In sub-Saharan Africa it is the leading cause of death among people living with HIV/AIDS. Like HIV/AIDS itself, TB thrives in conditions of community impoverishment (WHO, 2002b). However, the fragility of the public health infrastructure in most countries makes it difficult to respond to and control this disease, although well-tested methods of effective treatment are affordable.

The challenge posed by the HIV/AIDS epidemic and by the resurgence of TB and of other medical conditions is how to further shape health care systems to respond to individual and local needs. However, it is not simply a matter of reacting to conditions, but taking advantage of new or emerging therapies. In the context of HIV/AIDS, for example, health systems are expected to develop additional services to meet an expansion of treatment for those living with HIV/AIDS. Fortunately, some of those structures are already in place, such as voluntary counselling and testing (VCT) services. A study in Zambia found that half of VCT counsellors were non-health professionals and their performance was judged higher than all health practioners except nurses (Huddart et al., 2004).

The increasing affordability of antiretrovirals (ARVs) – the drugs to suppress HIV and the technical monitoring of the drugs' actions in people's bodies – offers hope for preventing hundreds of thousands of deaths each year. Effective use of ART requires trained medical personnel and appropriate equipment, and ensuring that people who need them have access to those resources. A study of health service provision in Zambia found that technical and management supervision of ART providers was inadequate due to the heavy workload of responsible staff (Huddart et al., 2004, pp. 26–7). The new requisites to treat HIV/AIDS add to the existing human resource constraints on most health systems and are a part of the rebuilding of fully functional health systems.

The HIV/AIDS epidemic has stimulated a number of creative and effective responses, some within the formal health care system and others created by civil society groups. In southern Zambia, for example, Chikankata Hospital and the communities within its catchment area evolved over several years an effective programme of community support for people and families living with HIV/AIDS, with medical back-up from the hospital staff. This was a complete turnaround from the programme initially begun by the hospital staff, where they provided much of the care. As the epidemic grew, the hospital staff could not meet the demands expected of their initial approach. Through discussions with community members, much day-to-day care and support devolved to the communities themselves, with ongoing training and support from the hospital. The system is not only affordable within existing resources, but stimulates communities to look at other problems that can be addressed through their initiatives (Silomba, 2002). The AIDS Support Organization (TASO), one of the earliest HIV/AIDS NGOs, which was established in Uganda, has demonstrated that 'home or community care is not about "decongestion of hospital beds" but about the provision of a comprehensive range of medical, nursing, counselling, spiritual as well as nutritional care which must exist from hospital to home, (continuum of care)' (Kaleeba et al., 2001, p. 15). Numerous other local models of patient and family care can be found across Africa to guide the creation or expansion of effective responses.

It will not be enough simply to train more medical and health personnel, improve working conditions and add new equipment. To adequately address what is known about the patterns of people living with HIV/AIDS and at risk of infection, health systems – and their role in national development – need to be reformed. What is evident is that because national responses to the HIV/AIDS epidemic have tended to follow international designs and financial assistance, health care services have focused on providing services for the care of PLWHA with known HIV status. In most countries the vast majority of people living with HIV infection do not know they are infected (Fylknes et al., 1999) and do not access the specialized services. Rather, according to the World Health Organization, general health care services provide the bulk of the care for most HIV-infected persons. Thus, the largest number of people with the need for HIV/AIDS services of all kinds do not, in most instances, have access to those services. As a consequence, 'national HIV/AIDS programme efforts to improve specific HIV/AIDS services rather than to support the general health service response to the needs of high HIV prevalence populations have run the risk of becoming specialized and elitist' (Gilks, 1998, p. 2; see also WHO, 2002b).

Health systems are an integral part of prevention and care in relation to the HIV/AIDS epidemic. National responses will not only focus on sustaining sector capacity and planning for future needs in terms of human resources; they will also address the sectoral imbalances that leave most people without access to knowledge of their HIV/AIDS status and without adequate and readily accessible services if they are infected. Thus, the health sector as it addresses HIV/AIDS will also address aspects of the inequalities that foster the spread of the disease.

Some of those reforms are underway. With international support, several countries are testing ways to more fully integrate public, private and community health services to deal with the broad range of HIV/AIDS and other health issues (WHO, 2002b, pp. 30–1). Especially through NGO and FBO initiatives, new cadres of community health workers are being trained, in Malawi, Uganda and Zambia, among other countries. In eastern and southern Africa – and to a lesser extent in west Africa – Ministries of Health have implemented or at least drafted HIV/AIDS workplace programmes for their own personnel (Gauteng Health Department in South Africa, 2002). Health systems themselves are adapting their training programmes, adding new skills and devolving certain responsibilities. Tanzania and other countries are reviewing the terms of service within the public service to improve conditions and retain personnel.

Contextualizing the Importance of Treatment for PLWHA

Treatment is often discussed as if it stood alone from other health and related issues, whereas it needs to be set within frameworks which are much more general if sensible decisions are to be made (see figure 4.1). Furthermore, the issues of access to treatment are not simply a matter of ARVs since there is a need to ensure that relatively inexpensive drugs are available for opportunistic infections such as TB and diarrhoea. In many countries access to drugs and other material inputs needed for effective care of those with HIV-related illnesses are generally not available for reasons often of resource constraints.[1]

Until recently, the provision of treatment was available only to a tiny fraction of HIV-positive people on the African continent. High costs, a demanding treatment regime and the lack of even a basic health infrastructure to deliver the treatment were cited as insurmountable barriers to providing treatment to Africans who needed it.

The reduction in the cost of ARVs and other drugs has significantly changed the possibilities for treatment of PLWHA, but it has also changed the potential for reducing the socio-economic cost of the epidemic to countries in Africa. It has done so in the following ways.

ARV treatment both directly reduces the infectivity of people and indirectly makes prevention programmes more

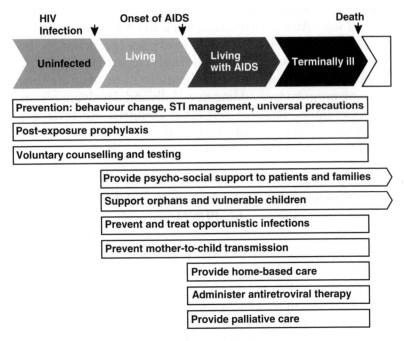

Figure 4.1 HIV/AIDS prevention and care continuum

effective by creating opportunities for effective treatment. This improves the probability that people with HIV, or those who think they may be HIV positive, will interact with counselling, VCT and other services, which constitutes an important step towards improving national prevention programmes. So treatment and prevention are linked in effectiveness, and not in competition for resources, at least not always, and not everywhere. These links to effective prevention activities have now been confirmed by many studies and it is evident that increasing access to treatment has the potential to transform the effectiveness of prevention activities, in part through widening access to VCT and in part through the mobilization of civil society organizations and communities.[2]

The costs of the epidemic to societies and economies are of course much greater than those usually quantified by economists, and so the benefits from treating people will also be greater, once there is a full accounting for the losses. These costs are to a significant degree socio-economic, and are largely avoidable through increasing access to treatment. Thus the costs of inactivity in conditions of weak access to treatment are much greater than the UNAIDS estimate of losses of 2.6 per cent of GDP annually, once all of the direct and indirect costs of the epidemic are factored into the analysis.

There is a separate and powerful case to be made in respect of access to ART for pregnant women where HIV transmission can be reduced substantially through the provision of mother-to-child transmission (MTCT) programmes that are relatively inexpensive and clearly beneficial to mothers and infants. The benefits are, of course, not confined to the direct beneficiaries but also accrue to society as a whole. Here the costs of drugs may not themselves be the main deterrent to their use, but rather issues relating to the infrastructure of testing and counselling, and other costs relating to the provision of treatment. Just as important for the success of MTCT programmes is the presence of an enabling framework of customs and social norms.

Thus in most countries in Africa even under the present cost conditions relating to the supply and delivery of ART, the total benefits undoubtedly exceed costs. This is true even in the poorest countries once there is a full calculation of all the benefits from increasing access to ART. The benefits from expanding access to treatment include the direct contributions to GDP of men and women who would otherwise have succumbed to morbidity and mortality, plus their unmeasured contributions in terms of social output. The social benefits also include those that arise from continued support to both young and elderly dependants, and in particular the avoidance of most of the social costs that arise from large and increasing numbers of orphans and vulnerable children.

Nevertheless current access to ARV treatment is in practice limited in most countries in Africa to those with higher incomes, although there are exceptions, such as the decision by Botswana to make ARVs available to all citizens. There are also increasing numbers of employers in the private sector who have calculated the private rate of return as being sufficiently large to make access to ARVs for employees (although not generally for family members) a worthwhile activity. In some companies the ART is provided at no cost, and in other cases there are counterpart charges placed on employees. Economists would argue that the costs of ART in both cases are effectively borne by wage-earners and should be seen as part of total labour compensation.

In general the provision of ART by companies is the exception and is often confined to very large enterprises such as Anglo Gold and Debswana, and to multinational companies such as Heineken and Daimler-Chrysler. But the response of governments in general has been to argue that there are budgetary constraints limiting access to ARV treatment, and that these constraints will continue for the foreseeable future. In taking this position they are probably right, in that the flows of additional resources needed to increase substantially access to ART may well exceed those likely to be available. But this pessimism is not entirely well founded and there are other factors involved that work in the opposite direction.

What level of financial costs are at issue here, and are national budget considerations so overwhelmingly negative? Estimates have been made by Geffen et al. (2003) of the costs of a publicly funded comprehensive programme in South Africa, including ARVs, costs of training, infrastructure improvements, and so on, and have concluded that it is feasible. They estimate that by 2015, the peak of projected expenditure, a comprehensive programme including prevention, treatment of opportunistic infections (OIs), ARVs, and so on, would cost 1.74 per cent of GNP – an increase in the share of health spending in GNP from 3.7 per cent to 5.4 per cent, with ART representing 99 per cent of the additional cost. At the present time it is estimated that 500,000 people need ARVs in South Africa but that fewer than 1,500 are actually receiving treatment. So the distance still to travel is substantial, but on the evidence it is achievable given leadership and resources.

Some of these additional financial costs are offset by reductions in expenditure on OIs and on hospital and related care, and savings in other areas of the budget (such as child welfare and other support for affected families). For example, very significant health resources are involved in the treatment of OIs, and ART leads to substantial savings of health resources given the rapid improvement in health status of patients in receipt of ARVs. Given that human resources are a major constraint on health provision generally, and not just for HIV-related illnesses, there are major gains from expanding access to ART simply through a reduction in OIs in the population.

There are major gains through the savings of time and drugs, and other resources, that follow from increasing access to ART. Thus data confirm that there are substantial reductions of OIs once patients are receiving ART and that very significant savings of resources are achievable – what economists refer to as 'opportunity cost savings'. The projected level of costs for ART are of course uncertain, but if recent trends are taken as indicators of the likely movement of financial costs, then they are certainly downward. The increasing availability of generic drugs for the treatment of OIs and ARVs has already caused sharp reductions in costs of programme delivery and there are possibilities for further reductions in prices. For example, a first-line generic ARV is now available for less than $135 per year which has an added advantage of being taken only twice a day, so reducing costs associated with adherence. Furthermore, there is some evidence that alternative treatment regimes, such as 'structured treatment interruption',[3] may yield additional reductions in the costs of ART (various pilots are presently underway in Africa to test these possibilities). There are other possible cost reductions on the horizon that relate to reductions in the costs of laboratory services (such as the price of CD4 and viral load tests), and improvements in other technologies relating to personal monitoring that are also cost-reducing.

Budgetary and other constraints are important, but it is essential at a minimum that the cost–benefit calculations accurately reflect the real choices for countries in Africa. The available evidence supports the argument that the total benefits from increasing access to ART exceed the full costs (drugs plus VCT, training and infrastructure investment, counselling and adherence costs, etc.) even in the poorest countries. Indeed, it can be easily demonstrated that the comparison of costs of access of ARV treatment relative to GDP per capita (as a measure of benefit) is a totally misleading one for policy makers.

In part the reason why such calculations produce the wrong answer is because they are too static, and need to become much more dynamic. On the face of it, in budget-constrained situations, if saving a life costs less by spending on malaria than in incurring annual costs over some unknown period on ARVs, then the choice may well lie with the former. But policy makers are facing an epidemic, which because of its scale is generating large socio-economic costs, both measurable and immeasurable, including higher levels of crime and insecurity, a worsening of economic performance, recurrent famines and mounting problems of food insecurity, increasing levels of poverty, and a widening of the income and wealth distributions. In these conditions the calculations of costs and benefits relating to access to treatment are totally changed, as also are the policy and programme options.

The problem is not that countries are facing budget constraints, for they are in all cases, but that they are wrongly assessing the choices that they face because they use methods that are inapplicable to epidemics that have become, or are about to become, generalized. The economic, social and political systems are fragile throughout the region, and AIDS has the capacity to destroy these over time. Indeed it is entirely unclear, for example, how Botswana could have coped with the predicted loss of 25 per cent of its total population (UNDP, 2000); similarly unknown futures also now face other countries in the region, such as Zimbabwe,

Swaziland, Lesotho and South Africa. The issues are not about the impact on GDP per capita, or even GDP in the aggregate, but rather how economic production can be sustained in the face of huge losses of social capital and productive capacity (Cohen, 2002).

Challenges to Scaling Up Treatment in Africa

It is estimated that only 400,000 HIV-infected persons in the developing countries currently receive ARVs of any kind – about half of them in Brazil alone (see table 4.2). The World Health Organization estimates that there are currently 100,000 people on ART in sub-Saharan Africa, a coverage of only 2 per cent, whilst over 4.4 million people remain in need of immediate treatment on the continent. The first funding commitments made by the Global Fund to Fight HIV/AIDS, Tuberculosis and Malaria in 2002 have allowed a two-fold increase in the total number of individuals receiving ART in developing countries, and a six-fold increase in Africa in the last few years.

Certain conditions can be identified as important in determining improved access to treatment for those living with HIV/AIDS. These vary in their importance in different countries but to a degree are present in all countries in sub-Saharan Africa. They are all amenable to policy and programme development, although some are more intractable than others. Even in countries where conditions for improving access to ART have appeared to be most favourable, such as Botswana, in practice strengthening access has proved to be much more difficult than was originally predicted. In 2005, some three years after the decision by the government of Botswana to widen access to ART, only 7,000 persons are enrolled in the programme. The reasons for the relative failure to scale up the programme in Botswana are complex, but this experience indicates that widening access to improved care and treatment will require action on many fronts if it is to be successful.

Table 4.2 Progress against '3 by 5' targets for numbers on ART, December 2004

WHO region	Estimated number of people receiving ART, December 2004 [low estimate–high estimate]	Estimated number of people 15–49 years old needing ART, 2004	ART, December 2004 (%)	Estimated number of people receiving ART, June 2004
African Region	310,000 [270,000–350,000]	4,000,000	8	150,000
Region of the Americas	275,000 [260,000–290,000]	425,000	65	220,000
European Region	15,000 [13,000–17,000]	150,000	10	11,000
Eastern Mediterranean	4,000 [2,000–6,000]	77,500	5	4,000
South-East Asia Region	85,000 [70,000–100,000]	950,000	9	40,000
Western Pacific Region	17,000 [15,000–19,000]	200,000	9	15,000
Total	700,000 [630,000–780,000]	5.8 million	12	440,000

Source: WHO, 2004

There is now mounting evidence from many countries in support of the proposition that increasing access to ART is feasible in resource-constrained settings, and that the direct financial costs of provision are not insurmountable – and are falling over time. The evidence from many pilot projects indicates that adherence is generally very high and that the effects on the health and quality of life of recipients is similar to that observed in the industrialized countries. As predicted, there are measurable and worthwhile social and economic benefits from ART as PLWHA are again able to resume their lives as productive members of society. These socio-economic benefits undoubtedly exceed in the aggregate the direct financial costs of providing ART and care.

But critical challenges remain in scaling up from current initiatives to the comprehensive treatment programmes needed in Africa. These challenges can be broadly grouped into two categories: *challenges related to demand and challenges related to supply*. The demand-side challenges are associated with the unprecedented large burden of advanced disease, the dangerous ensuing patient presentation profiles, and the incredibly constrained timeframes within which interventions must yield the required impact. The supply-side challenges are associated with the logistical challenges of tackling this massive demand in the context of the existing deficits in political will, health systems (including leadership and management), human resources, technical expertise, physical infrastructure, equipment and supplies. A third broad category of challenge that cuts across both the demand and the supply sides is that related to 'stakeholder buy-in': commitment from the range of key stakeholders that need to be involved to ensure successful programme implementation and appropriate timely uptake of relevant services (including treatment).

Demand-Side Challenges

These are challenges peculiar to the population that needs to be reached. These include: (a) a large burden of disease, which, due to magnitude alone, poses numerous logic-defying challenges that cannot be addressed by existing health care capacity and models of care in most African countries; (b) an advanced epidemic with a relatively large cohort of critically ill (or soon to be critically ill), which in turn imposes critically ill patients with exponentially higher resource and care needs on already overburdened and under-staffed health facilities; (c) very little programme maturity time within which new initiatives have to build the required capacity and deliver results (race against time).

Low levels of knowledge of HIV status The vast majority of those who require services are still 'unidentifiable' because, despite the dreadful high-prevalence statistics, most individuals do not know their HIV status (be it positive or negative). Because knowledge of status is the critical entry point for any type of services, lack of knowledge in turn means that, all things being equal, individuals tend only to be identified once they have to interact with the health establishment. Usually this is due to illness (meaning low CD4 counts), and thus ART becomes emergency intervention which further stresses scarce resources. Worse yet, individuals who are diagnosed at a late stage have in most cases already lost their livelihood/employment, and even if therapy is successful, they become wards of the state with their families.

Development of non-virtuous feedback loops in patient queues The natural triage that occurs at the point of care whereby the most severely ill are prioritized further contributes to the creation of functional bottlenecks because the sickest patients require the most time, and when imposed on small numbers of newly trained staff, queues begin to form. This can result in a negative spiral of ever-increasing insatiable demand where the *de facto* eligibility criterion that gets someone to the front of the line is 'being nearest the point of death'.

Maintenance of high adherence levels Appropriate treatment with ARVs results in dramatic improvement of clinical status, but the nature of the HIV virus and the need to minimize development of its resistance to drugs demand high levels of adherence. This then creates a high follow-up burden that the health system must invest in and sustain.

Fear and stigma As more treatment programmes are initiated, evidence is emerging that the availability of treatment serves as a powerful incentive for testing (and to empower health workers to be more proactive in testing). The long legacy of absence of ART fostered and embedded a sense of hopelessness in communities (and in many cases apathy within the health system) which in turn provided fertile ground for fear and stigma to take root. Fear of testing and stigma therefore present conceptual and emotional barriers which prevent access to services. Programmes and initiatives must address these daunting issues as they race against time.

Traditional medicine and beliefs and language Traditional medicine and beliefs abound in many African countries and have served a critical need for large portions of African populations. However, in the case of HIV/AIDS traditional belief systems may run counter to the desired paradigms of allopathic medical practice, resulting in a 'tug of war' for patients which occasionally results in losing critical time before accessing ART or discontinuing therapy after commencing. The multiplicity of languages and dialects also poses a particular challenge to providing information, education and culturally appropriate communication which has the intended effect.

Supply-Side Challenges

In the African context, limited human, physical and financial resources represent major barriers to scaling up treatment provision. It must be noted that most African countries had severe capacity constraints and were not meeting the health needs of their populations long before HIV/AIDS even existed. The capacity deficit is therefore all the more acute with the imposition of HIV/AIDS. Countries are therefore in the position whereby they must address many decades of underdevelopment (of their entire health systems) within extremely short timeframes if they are to save the lives required and adequately service their populations. The main barriers are as follows:

Models of care with intrinsically low scalability The vast majority of African countries utilize the Western referral model of care, which tends to require large numbers of specialized health workers. Whereas such models are appropriate to address conditions that occur in relatively low prevalence, the burden associated with HIV management is so large that such models become untenable. Furthermore, high degrees of staff role definitions (often defined policy and schemes of service) and 'verticalization' of programmes (often development-partner-driven) create redundancy and duplication which contribute to a functional decrease in effective available staff capacity. The reality is that patients will spend the greatest proportion of their lives in communities and not in the confines of health facilities; therefore the challenge is how to maintain large numbers of community-based individuals on long-term therapy with high adherence and compliance.

Unfortunately many intervention efforts tend to grow around health centres as opposed to the community where the target audience actually is. Large-scale integrated public health models for addressing ART at the primary care and community level are unfortunately lacking and urgently need to be developed. Accordingly, decision makers and leaders of health systems must be willing to make some hard choices (which may require policy change, difficult redefinition and devolution of roles and schemes of service, and review of professional licensure and accreditation requirements) and institute simplified public health models which use alternative providers (under supervision) where everyone down to the level of infected and affected individuals plays a role as part of an extended health team. Technology offers many new and exciting possibilities for leveraging rare skills and expertise over large numbers of mid-level and alternative health providers, and these options need to be investigated (see box 4.1). Mobile extension health service models need to be refined, adapted and used to extend ART into communities and across widely dispersed geographies.

Inadequate (and declining) human resources for delivering ART
In addition to optimizing the models of care (ideally as a key priority and prerequisite), an immediate imperative is to stabilize and replenish the existing human resource base that provides health care in Africa. In many countries, that base is under siege. Health providers themselves are getting sick at high rates, and many who are healthy are migrating out in search of socio-economic and professional betterment. Furthermore, ART requires close supervision and monitoring of the patient's compliance to treatment. This requires

---

Box 4.1 Innovative Ways of Coping with the Challenge of Introducing ARVs

Botswana is developing new cadres planning to train and employ 500 lay counsellors.

Malawi is considering new approaches: for example, reducing the frequency of monitoring visits for stable and adherent patients, prescribing of ARVs by district hospitals with collection of drugs and monitoring at satellite health centres using simplified clinical review guidelines, and developing simple but robust record-keeping and drug-monitoring systems.

Kenya and Uganda are reconsidering the skill mix: reducing dependence on highly trained physicians and training clinical officers to perform more routine functions associated with the provision of ART.

substantial work-time from medical staff. Lack of availability of antiretrovirals on the continent meant that most health providers were not trained on how to deliver ART and relevant supportive, logistical and monitoring services.

In a recent Kenyan study, for example, it was shown that whilst doctors throughout the country were prescribing antiretroviral drugs, only 30 per cent of these doctors had received any training in administering and monitoring ART. There is a clear need to develop rapid training methodologies as training represents the key rate-limiting step to the commencement of services across all cadres that will be involved in ART. The large logistical burden of addressing HIV/AIDS demands that health workers (and others) become adept at leadership, planning and project management to optimize use of existing resources and manage workflows in a manner that maximizes patient flow and minimizes dangerous queuing. These skill sets are severely lacking in the health establishment and need to be a critical component of the training. It is also necessary to improve motivation, working environments and incentives. Tackling issues such as low remuneration and poor benefits, insufficient infrastructure and lack of opportunities for career development is a prime challenge in preventing migration of health professionals and improving an enabling environment for AIDS treatment and care. Programme implementers must also tackle very practical issues associated with the reluctance of many health workers to go to very rural locations (lack of services, schools for children, amenities and conveniences) as well as lack of housing (in urban and rural settings alike).

Pilot projects have shown that some tasks related to ART, such as routine follow-ups and counselling, can be carried out by lay community workers, properly trained and supported by referral systems. Scaling up ART therefore also poses the challenge of training and managing more community workers to ease the burden of medical personnel.

Lack of financial capacity Costs of ARVs have declined substantially, but the price is still prohibitive for most Africans.

Take the example of Kenya, where, even under the best-case scenario of ARVs becoming available at $1 per day, they would cost 100 per cent of the average monthly income of $30. At the national level, treating 25 per cent of all HIV-infected individuals in Kenya would cost 6.3 per cent of GNP, more than seven times the current government spending on health. For scaling up to be successful, the price of ART and related interventions will need to come down to the level where African governments can budget for them in a sustainable manner.

A number of recent international initiatives provide funding for scaling up AIDS treatment in Africa. Key initiatives for AIDS treatment in Africa such as the Global Fund, the Bill and Melinda Gates Foundation and President Bush's AIDS Initiative represent very positive developments, but have a limited life span. A challenge for governments is that once started, ART must be provided for the patient's lifetime. When the international funding dries up, governments need to find a way to foot the bill. Improving sustainability and predictability of funds is therefore key to ensuring life-long access treatment. Governments are also faced with the challenge to reduce dependency on external funding by increasing domestic resources and investing donors' resources in capital rather than recurrent costs.

Another challenge for a number of African governments is to increase absorptive capacity to funnel the additional funding appropriately through the public expenditure framework. External criteria such as maximum levels (or 'ceilings') on public spending imposed by international financial institutions (such as the IMF) in order to safeguard macro-economic stability at times creates major obstacles. In addition, in-country financial processing, disbursement, auditing and overall management tend to be either bureaucratic, complex, underdeveloped, insecure or all of these. As a result, countries have found themselves either unable to accept or unable rapidly to deploy additional funding for HIV/AIDS. This issue needs to be addressed in a consistent manner. In addition, governments are required to expand their absorptive capacity to enable utilization of increasing external funds for health.

In any case, cost considerations of treatment should not hinder the promotion of treatment. The provision of treatment is, ultimately, a cost-saving strategy. The benefits of providing treatment, through averted hospitalization costs, the social benefits in terms of maintaining household cohesion and saving children from orphanhood, and the economic benefits of maintaining the workforce, are estimated to exceed the financial costs of providing treatment.

Inadequate laboratory and patient care infrastructure ART is a complex process which requires close surveillance by care providers, careful adherence to the therapeutic regime, and access to laboratory facilities for continual testing so that the progress of therapy can be monitored and adjusted as necessary. Adequate laboratory and testing facilities must be available if ART programmes are to be undertaken successfully. In a recent Kenyan study, for example, it was shown that outside Nairobi, no laboratory facilities were available for monitoring the progress of therapy. Wide geographic distribution of patients and poor transportation networks necessitate the development and deployment of simple technologies with adequate sensitivity and specificity which can be used in severely resource-constrained environments by non-specialized personnel. Concerted international effort is needed in this regard to explore and research simple technologies that give 'good-enough' measures for public health programmes (e.g. a simplified test based on a colour-changing strip which indicates whether a patient has fewer than 200 CD4 cells/mm^3, at which point treatment should begin, according to WHO treatment guidelines).

Poor patient follow-up leading to low adherence Patients must take ARVs on a regular basis. If random interruptions occur, the virus is likely to mutate into drug-resistant strains. Lack of adherence to treatment is not a new problem. For example, the emergence of multi-drug-resistant TB is related to lack of adherence to TB treatment. ART, as a life-long, complex and time-demanding treatment, complicates adherence. This is compounded by the stigma surrounding AIDS, forcing some patients to follow the treatment secretly. Close patient follow-up has been shown to increase adherence, but this is a challenge in resource-constrained African settings where traditionally follow-up systems have been either absent or poor at best. Experience from Botswana reveals that paper-based systems of monitoring and follow-up work well when the numbers of patients are relatively small. As the numbers increase into the thousands, however, paper-based systems become increasingly inadequate to deal with the large information needs and interchanges associated with follow-up (transferring laboratory results, patient referrals, monitoring drop-outs, prescription pick-ups, side-effects, clinical parameters, programme logistics, etc.). Thus a combination of paper and electronic systems may become necessary. For countries that embark on operating electronic data systems, such an endeavour will require equipping staff at all levels with computer literacy and software-specific skills, which adds to the training burden and the time necessary to prepare health workers to be fully functional.

Sustainable drug supply A discontinuation in drug supply increases the risk of treatment failure. This is not only detrimental to the patient, but also facilitates the emergence of drug-resistant strains of the virus. Periodic drug shortages are not uncommon in Africa, as, for example, the shortages denounced by Médécins sans Frontières (MSF) and the World Health Organization in Kenya in 2003. The challenge at the national level is to build strong drug procurement and distribution systems, avoiding supply interruptions as well as leakages of drugs, and ensuring drug quality. At the project level, logistics are also crucial, including mechanisms to ensure safe drug storage and distribution. There are also challenges associated with lack of availability of adequate formulations for children, and in-country registration procedures and requirements need to be simplified and streamlined for the efficient and rapid introduction of new drugs.

Fostering Stakeholder Buy-In

Involvement from all stakeholders will be key if the scale of efforts is ever to reach the levels necessary to conquer the HIV/AIDS pandemic. An overarching challenge associated with generating, sustaining and appropriately directing stakeholder buy-in is the issue of co-ordination. Increased funding levels for HIV/AIDS have naturally generated a dramatic increase in service agencies, which all need to demonstrate their unique value in the field. This at times leads to wasteful duplication, lack of co-operation, inefficient misdirected programming and non-attainment of results. Countries must take leadership and responsibility for defining the strategic frameworks for their national responses and co-ordinate the participation of all key stakeholders within them. Most importantly, all implementers must be strictly held accountable for results and, as much as possible, funding should be based on actual performance. Successful scaling up of treatment requires not only adequate health care infrastructure, but also commitment and leadership at all levels.

Private sector, NGO and FBO involvement Currently, both the private sector, NGOs and FBOs (including mission hospitals) have been in the front line of treatment provision in sub-Saharan Africa. As ART is increasingly made available through the public health care systems, efficient co-ordination and harnessing of the whole spectrum of providers will be crucial. The growing role of the private sector calls for stronger partnerships and endorsed collaborative frameworks between public and private sectors in order to ensure quality and equity of services. Workplaces, established networks of people and institutions are organizing units that give a unique opportunity to offer targeted interventions to identifiable 'captive' audiences. The opportunities afforded by such settings must be capitalized on.

Community involvement Community involvement is crucial to scaling up treatment, for three main reasons. First, communities are instrumental in fighting against stigma and advocating for treatment. Second, their involvement is key in identifying eligibility criteria for treatment. Third, communities are also required to care and support for the infected individuals (including adherence support) and affected families. Already strained by multiple demands, communities in the hardest-hit areas are struggling to cope. More research needs to be devoted to finding out how best to equip communities and maximize their capacity to address these challenges while maintaining community cohesion. Optimization and use of existing community-based organizations (CBOs), leadership and authority structures need to be actively explored to avoid creation of expensive, redundant and possibly ineffective interventions. A key question is how to maintain active engagement at all levels of the process, ensuring that growing responsibilities are accompanied by the necessary tools and resources for implementation.

Ensuring family and individual involvement The greatest challenge associated with ART is adherence. This means that the individual on ART and those surrounding him or her become the most important 'human resources' in the equation. Early programmatic experience indicates that it is critical that all individuals develop a sense of responsibility for themselves and their care. Governments and organizations can only help if individuals likewise rise to the occasion and view the HIV/AIDS epidemic as their own emergency on a personal level. First and foremost, individuals must invest in their own health. It is therefore critical that all individuals be equipped with tools, skills, knowledge and resources either to stay negative or, if positive, to take steps proactively to seek services at the appropriate time, manage their medications appropriately and partake in positive living and wellness-promoting activities. There is an urgent need to explore the role of targeted skills-based mass education programming as well as to develop effective contextually and culturally appropriate tools for population- and community-level information, education and communication tools, modalities and methodologies. These are the critical ingredients of behaviour change and ART demands significant behaviour change. As such, the communication and education component of an ART programme is a key backbone issue, which, if not developed and managed properly, can lead to its collapse. Unfortunately, communication and public education efforts are often viewed as an 'afterthought'. However, this issue must be brought to the forefront as one of the most important and critical programmatic interventions which deserves significant budgeting and resource consideration.

Ensuring equitable access to treatment and care Access to treatment and care is a human right. However, in contexts where the need for treatment exceeds the available supply, health care providers have to tackle the difficult question of who gets access to life-saving services and why. Human rights, law and ethics provide guidance to expanding services in a just and equitable manner. Principles of *utility*, *efficiency*, *fairness* and *sustainability* need to be incorporated and balanced on a case-by-case basis. Involving stakeholders has emerged as a way to facilitate transparent decision-making processes. Experience on prioritization in resource-limited settings is evolving. Botswana, for example, has developed an interesting prioritization guideline that only kicks in when resource constraints force the health provider to make a choice (at the margin). If a choice needs to be made, children, HIV positive women and their spouses, and patients with active TB get prioritized. MSF in South Africa establishes eligibility based on biomedical adherence and social criteria.

Need to address social and cultural barriers to testing One of the first lessons from the 'Masa' (new dawn) programme in Botswana, which constituted the first widespread distribution of ARVs through the public health system in Africa, is that initially, significantly fewer people than expected were coming forward for testing despite the documented high prevalence rates in the country. The ART sites were overwhelmed due to the very sick patients who came forward first (and the fact that initially there were few sites and few trained health providers) but the numbers in the queue were far short of the numbers who should have been in the queue given the prevalence and advanced stage of the epidemic. This dynamic revealed what in essence is likely to be the greatest initial challenge Africa will face in reaching and treating the individuals who need services before it is too late – the vast majority of individuals, including those who are in health facilities, who do not know their HIV status and have not been motivated to find it out on their own accord. There are numerous factors that probably contribute to this widespread lack of knowledge of status. First and foremost is the natural human tendency only to seek health services when something feels wrong. Fear seems to be a primary factor that keeps most individuals who feel fine from proactively testing. Once diagnosed as HIV positive, stigma and discrimination then pose additional psycho-social challenges to appropriate access and utilization of services (where they exist). Ultimately it is hoped that the availability of ART will go a long way towards normalizing HIV/AIDS as a manageable chronic disease. However, much work needs to be done to reverse many decades where poor information (HIV was introduced as an 'immoral' disease early in its discovery), compounded by lack of options and services in Africa, fed the flames of fear and stigma to the current levels. Much more therefore needs to be done to overcome the psychosocial and cultural constraints on treatment.

Case Study I: Learning the Lessons of Botswana's Experience[4]

Situation Analysis

In interpreting the experience of Botswana for other countries in Africa it is important to recall some of the factors that make it an untypical country. It is a middle-income country which has made remarkable progress in human development since independence. The development of the country has been genuinely transformative, largely based on the wise use of the resources generated by the diamond sector. It is now a thriving economy with excellent access to key public services such as education and health, a good transport and communications system, and is characterized by inclusive and democratic political institutions.

Botswana is in many senses no longer a rural society, and most of the population of 1.6 million is effectively urban or peri-urban. It is nevertheless still a country with wide income inequality, and some 60 per cent of the population are classified as living in poverty. The poverty and high mobility of the population are clearly factors in the high levels of HIV prevalence that exist (approx. 36 per cent of adults infected with HIV). But it remains a central task for policy effectively to address the socio-economic structural factors of poverty and gender that are driving the epidemic. This is despite the fact that Botswana has invested heavily in health and education and was an early adopter of a multi-sectoral response to the epidemic.

Botswana is therefore to a significant degree untypical; a small country in terms of population, and one that is increasingly urbanized and relatively easy to access through effective public services such as education, health, social welfare, and so on. It has experienced a rapid growth in HIV prevalence from relatively low levels in the early 1990s to the very high level observed today. It is worth noting that the gap between urban and rural HIV prevalence is relatively small, which is very untypical of most countries in Africa.

At the present time Botswana has ample financial resources to address the issues raised by HIV/AIDS, including the decision to make ART generally available for free to all Botswanans. But it is constrained in terms of its ability to achieve its policy targets by human resources that remain scarce in many critical areas despite the investment in education and training. HIV/AIDS has the effect of exacerbating this long-term problem of shortages of human resources due to its impact on morbidity and mortality. Furthermore, Botswana is a country where stigma and discrimination against PLWHA and their families are deeply embedded in the population, and this has enormous implications for the ability to increase access to care and treatment.

Programme Review

The estimate of the population in need of access to ART is necessarily somewhat arbitrary but was assumed to be around 110,000 adults and children (30 per cent of the total of HIV positive of 290,000 with CD4 counts of less than 200, plus an estimated 10 per cent of the total who are symptomatic with CD4s in excess of 200). There are four target groups: pregnant women and their partners; adult inpatients; paediatric patients; and TB patients. Services were planned to be at four selected urban sites and two district hospitals and it was the aim to build capacity to treat 19,000 people in the first year of operation. Delivery of treatment depended on upgrading the health system, establishing specialized labs for viral load and CD4 measurement, and strengthening personnel (doctors, nurses, pharmacists, lay counsellors, etc.). Processes were established to ensure compliance and monitoring, including CD4 count and viral load tests that are undertaken at regular intervals.

The system established is comprehensive and intensive in terms of both financial and human resources. In developing

the programme Botswana was assisted by international partners such as the African Comprehensive HIV/AIDS Partnerships (ACHAP), the Harvard AIDS Institute and the
Centres for Disease Control and Prevention (CDC). It is
worth noting in this regard that there are long-term financial
implications of the programme that will ultimately have to
be met by the government of Botswana, such that sustainability is a relevant consideration that needs to be taken into
account.

The current status of the programme is that about 7,000
patients are receiving treatment, and that some 90 per cent
are responding. One feature that was largely unanticipated
is that patients are often sicker then expected, with CD4
counts that are often very low (the average at enrolment is
50). While all the initial sites are operational, after a fairly significant delay, it is still the case that while patient demand is
well below the estimated need it is still greater than capacity.
The result is that many fewer patients are receiving treatment
than planned, and that even so there are significant waiting
times at the various sites (of the order of six months).

Learning the Lessons

These can be relatively easily summarized as follows:

- an ongoing lack of physical infrastructure that will require
  further investment to meet the demands falling on the
  system;
- continuing shortages of human resources of all kinds –
  doctors, nurses, pharmacists and technicians, trained
  counsellors, and so on;
- problems with tracking patients and very limited community involvement in the provision of treatment and
  monitoring and support to patients.

Inevitably these problems with capacity raise issues with
respect to the target groups (who should be treated) and how
to manage the queues that have developed already because

of the relative slowness in developing capacity. It seems clear that there will have to be a significant redesign of the programme in terms of the roles played by professionals if ARV treatment is to be rapidly extended to those in need. This will mean substituting less expensive human resources (nurses mainly) for more expensive ones (doctors), and a greater use of less intensively trained personnel in areas of care and counselling. Botswana is in the process of setting up a medical school but it will be years before there is any significant increase in trained human resources.

The greater the delay in treating patients (the longer the queues), the more patients will present themselves who are very sick and the greater the expenditures per patient. This further reduces the capacity to treat patients, and thus the queues lengthen. Hence the need to increase current access if these problems are to be avoided, but this means rapidly expanding the present capacity. In part this means more physical infrastructure, in part it means redefining the roles and competences of professional labour, and in part it means expanding community involvement. None of these changes will be easy to achieve, but they are essential if access to treatment and care is to be expanded.

Certain broader lessons stand out:

- It is certainly feasible to set up and expand access to ARV treatment provided the financial and other resources are present. But even under very favourable circumstances in these respects, such as those in Botswana, there are real problems in increasing access to treatment at all rapidly.
- Nevertheless, the experience of Botswana shows that it is feasible to provide ARV treatment through the public sector to the great benefit of patients. These benefits are present despite the low average level of CD4 counts for most patients at the initial stage, and most patients do respond well to ART.
- But slowness in generating the required capacity inevitably leads to queues, and this has downstream consequences for the system's capacity to cope with the

number of patients who are in need of treatment. This means addressing the issue of how best to expand capacity, and looking afresh at opportunities for providing services in less resource-intensive ways.

- Scaling up access to treatment inevitably entails addressing difficult issues relating to the competencies and use of professional and lay human resources so as to maximize the benefits for everyone. It follows that processes need to be in place to resolve issues of conflict with respect to important areas relating to professional activities of health sector workers – including the appropriate use of lay persons in the provision of care, support and treatment.

- It is also evident that strengthening access to treatment is not simply a matter for professionals but must in addition involve communities. The high levels of stigma and discrimination help to explain the slow progress. This has been especially important for women and in part explains the slow progress with MTCT activities, where significant levels of refusal of treatment have been witnessed even where conditions relating to access are extremely favourable.

One of the most difficult choices that needs to be made relates to targeting treatment, where, because of the slowness in expanding access, it is imperative that those with the greatest need are prioritized. But there is a potential here for conflict between the needs of individuals and what might be optimal for society and the economy. Should, for example, resources be focused on those with key economic roles where sustaining productive capacity may be seen as overriding other concerns? There are no simple rules to deal with these difficult decisions, but, given the inevitable slowness in increasing access to treatment and care, there will be choices that will have to be made. In part the question is about processes for making decisions on who receives treatment, and the need to ensure that these are open and transparent.

Case Study II: The Challenge of Scaling Up Care and Treatment for PLWHA in Mozambique

Situation Analysis

Mozambique provides a good contrast to Botswana in that in spite of impressive recent growth rates, the country remains among the less developed countries in the world, with a GDP per capita of $200 in 2001, and a Human Development Index (HDI) score of 0.356 in 2003 (ranking 170 of 175). The HDI has risen in absolute terms in recent years, reflecting the improved growth performance of the economy and reductions in illiteracy, but the development performance continues to be highly skewed. Against this background, HIV/AIDS has been accelerating with increasing intensity. There are currently an estimated 1.5 million people living with HIV or AIDS in the country, constituting a prevalence rate of 13.6 per cent (721,803 male and 920,130 female). In the next three years this figure will reach 1.8 million and the number of orphans, now estimated to be more than 300,000, will also escalate to 900,000 by the end of 2010 (INE, 2002). The prospect of increased resources coupled with the decreasing costs of ART provides an opportunity to scale up the national response, but it also presents enormous challenges due to the lack of adequate financial, human, technical and institutional capacities at all levels. Some of the challenges for scaling up care and treatment are listed below.

There are 17,000 health workers in Mozambique, of whom 11,000 are trained. Only 6 per cent are doctors; consequently less than 50 per cent of the districts have a doctor. Until now, a very small number of doctors have been credited to prescribe antiretroviral treatment. The number of doctors and nurses per patient is very low compared with other African countries. For instance, the number of nurses per patient is 1 : 1,298 in Malawi, 1 : 704 in Zimbabwe, 1 : 610 in Zambia, 1 : 457 in Botswana and 1 : 215 in South Africa, while in Mozambique it is 1 : 5,000.

The number of counsellors and pharmacists is limited. Counsellors have been trained incrementally according to the number of VCT centres opened, and there are not enough to cover the whole National Health Service. To overcome the insufficient number of pharmacists, middle, basic and elementary levels of pharmacy cadres have been trained. However, these cadres cannot replace the pharmacists, whose responsibilities include supervising the work of the team, defining procedures and controlling the quality of the drugs. There are now fourteen pharmacists in the National Health Service and Ministry of Health and twenty-four in the private sector. Twelve more pharmacists are expected to graduate by November 2005 to reinforce the workforce. It is, however, clear that these numbers are insufficient and many more pharmacists are needed.

Annually the districts lose 7 per cent of their staff, mainly due to transfers or death. A study was conducted and showed that 10–15 per cent of staff could die from AIDS between 2002 and 2010 (Ministério da Saúde, 2003a). Another important conclusion from the same study was that the level of knowledge on AIDS was very low in all ranks of health workers. The study concluded that most health workers are neither able to give good information to patients and the public in general, nor able to treat OIs properly. Continuing education is therefore vital.

The management of human resources needs more attention as there are bureaucratic procedures in the government hampering the posting of staff; sometimes it can take months before workers are put on the payroll. There is also a general lack of motivation in the workforce due to a myriad of small issues that are not addressed. In relation to salaries, it is believed that they are paid well below their market rate. Some provinces have started an incentive programme in order to retain health personnel, especially those who are more marketable.

Although the health system in Mozambique comprises a private and a public sector, the latter is the main health provider at the national level. The quality of care it provides is hampered by: the minimal qualifications of health personnel situated in the remote areas; chronic moral erosion and low motivation and professional ethics resulting from difficult working conditions, difficult living conditions and low salaries; poorly maintained infrastructures and deficient hygienic conditions; no or badly maintained equipment; deficient supervision from higher levels and low quality perception from users.

The health network is composed of 1,000 units, where more than 50 per cent are health posts with limited provision of services. There are 400 maternity wards, where less than 10 per cent provide basic emergency obstetric care. Around 200 health units have laboratory facilities, but more than 75 per cent of them are mini-labs, equipped with very basic equipment and personnel. The provinces of Nampula and Zambezia (in northern Mozambique) are the country's most populated, with the fewest number of beds per 1,000 people. The avalanche of HIV/AIDS patients take up most of the beds, and other patients have to be discharged to give room.

The laboratories in the hospitals and health centres are not equipped to test those in need as the tests are prioritized towards blood donors. Others who seek testing have to use the VCT centres, which are sometimes situated outside hospital premises. Therefore, handling the increased demand as a result of HIV/AIDS will require substantial strengthening of services. This includes management of drug procurement and distribution, rehabilitation and expansion of the physical infrastructure, acquisition of equipment and supplies, and improvement of laboratories.

Programme Review

The number of patients who are presumed to be in immediate need of ART is 54,000, but fewer than 2000 are currently undergoing treatment (Ministério da Saúde, 2003b). Up to 2002, there was no mention of ART. The new National

Strategic Plan (NSP) covering the period 2004–8 presents a more comprehensive list of services, namely:

- ART centres;
- laboratories for CD4 and viral load measurements – only three in existence: two in Maputo and one in Beira;
- day hospitals;
- youth- and adolescent-friendly services;
- prevention of mother-to-child transmission;
- home-based care.

These services only cover a very small geographical area of the country. The youth- and adolescent-friendly services provide several services related to reproductive health, counselling and testing. From 2000 to 2002 a total of 55,591 adolescent and young people aged 10–24 years used these services, of whom only 18 per cent were male (Ministério da Saúde, 2003b). No health unit has equipment for serologic diagnosis of HIV/AIDS, much less for the lab diagnosis of the majority of the OIs. The treatment of these diseases has been difficult partially due to the insufficient training and experience of the majority of technicians and pharmaceuticals.

The Pharmaceutical Department estimates that an increase of 40 per cent of antibiotics is needed for treatment of OIs. Since there are no additional funds to cover this need, it has not yet been translated into action. The promise of funds, namely from the Global Fund, the World Bank's Multi-country HIV/AIDS Programme (MAP) and the Bill Clinton Foundation, committed to provide more than $300 million by 2010, led to the design of the current NSP. These funds will allow provision of ART, and improve the National Health Service and systems.

The population has limited access to health services, with the population from towns benefiting more in comparison to those from the rural areas. Less than 40 per cent of the population have access to health services and fewer than 50 per cent of births are attended by skilled personnel. The roads and means of transportation available in some areas of the country do not allow proper communication to/from health centres. The number of people diagnosed and treated is still only a fraction of those actually needing treatment. Those treated come mainly from urban settings rather than the rural areas, where 80 per cent of the population lives (INE, 2002).

The Integrated Network provides the basic infrastructure of care, and includes in its network day clinics, VCT, treatment of OIs and chemoprophilaxy, as well as ART. It links the different services, including the tuberculosis programme, the prevention of MTCT programme and home-based care. Presently, the day clinics are located in urban centres. In 2004 fourteen day clinics were providing treatment within the Integrated Network. In 2005–6, the country plans to open an additional ten day clinics. These clinics will provide ART for an estimated 8,000 patients in 2005, and increase to 132,280 patients in 2008, according to the Ministry of Health. The health units are estimated to receive 100,000 new patients with AIDS annually, requiring 1.5 million consultations and around 3 million days in hospital, leading to an enormous strain on the system (CHGA, 2004d).

Case Study III: The Khayelitsha Programme in South Africa

Situation Analysis

South Africa has over 5 million people infected with HIV/AIDS, which is more than any other country globally. It has sought to put in place comprehensive programmes for prevention, care and mitigation of the socio-economic impact of the epidemic, and has been at the forefront in recent years of developing and implementing broad-based workplace programmes in both the private and public sectors. It has, nevertheless, lagged behind some countries in Africa in increasing access to ART, and government has until very recently been unresponsive to demands that ART be made available through public programmes. Public policy is now fully supportive of increasing access to ART, and the stage is now set of a rapid scaling up of access to treatment within integrated public health systems. There remain, however, major challenges, some of which are noted below.

Since 1999 MSF has been operating in the Khayelitsha township in Cape Town, initially in support of a provincial MTCT programme. The township is poor and has an estimated 500,000 inhabitants. About 50 per cent of adults are unemployed and housing and other social conditions are very unfavourable. The rate of HIV amongst pregnant women is 25 per cent, which suggests that about 50,000 residents are infected with HIV. In April 2000 MSF in collaboration with the provincial government set up three HIV/AIDS clinics within the Primary Health System, and in May 2002 began to offer ARV treatment to people with an advanced stage of HIV infection. The aim of the programme was two-fold:

- to demonstrate that ARV treatment is both feasible and effective in a primary health care setting and under resource-constrained conditions; and
- to prove that poor countries can provide affordable ARV treatment through the provision of low-cost drugs and to provide a model of a programme that was replicable in similar conditions.

Programme Review

The three clinics are situated within community centres and provide a full range of AIDS services, including counselling, treatment of OIs, ARV treatment, and so on. It is serviced by a team of health professionals which over time has shifted in terms of balance towards more nurse-based services, which are considered to be more easily replicated elsewhere in Africa. The clinics have been servicing some 1,800 patients each month, with varying regularity of visits depending on patient needs.

Very great care was taken in establishing eligibility for treatment given the excess demand conditions present in the community for ART. The criteria applied were clinical, social and also geographic. Only people who attend the clinics regularly and live in the community were considered for treatment. Once eligibility in terms of clinical status had been satisfied, a social worker then assessed the social and other support structures available in the home environment, including confirmation that at least one person was aware of the person's HIV status and would assist with treatment.

When these conditions had been established, there was then an anonymous enrolment process undertaken by independent clinicians and members of the community that took into account all relevant information. In reaching decisions on enrolment, criteria considered included number of dependants, health status, income, disclosure of HIV status and activism on HIV in the community. The very sick and the poor were given preference in the selection process.

Once selected, the person was given appropriate lab tests, and on the basis of these treatment was started using standard triple-therapy regimes. Progress was regularly monitored and tests were undertaken by the National Health Service Laboratory services. The clinical outcomes have been startlingly successful, and after six months 88 per cent of those on ARVs had undetectable viral load levels, and 83 per cent had sustained viral load suppression after a year. The pilot concluded that, 'Over time the health-related quality of life of those on treatment approached that of the community sample in all domains, until at 6 months the ARV treatment and community populations did not differ significantly. . . . Survival at 18 months was 84 per cent' (WHO, 2003, p. 2).

Adherence to the treatment regime was exceptionally high, and this in part reflected the fact that MSF ensured that the various strategic conditions were satisfied. These included simplified and standardized treatment regimes that minimize the pressures on patients, together with patient-centred education to ensure understanding of the treatment regime under strong support conditions from individuals and from specially constituted AIDS support groups. The pilot concluded as follows: 'Combining simplified regimes with a low pill burden and a comprehensive support programme, beneficiaries of the Khayelitsha ARV treatment programme show high levels of adherence to the medication' (WHO, 2003, p. 3).

This programme is part of a comprehensive set of prevention activities undertaken in the Western Cape in recent years that includes VCT, youth clinics, MTCT programmes, and so on. The provision of all these services together with public education about HIV/AIDS has been an essential part of the creation of a supportive environment within the Province. Thus it is not perhaps surprising that a survey of HIV prevention behaviour and practice in nine commuter sites in South Africa in 2002 found that Khayelitsha had the highest levels of condom use, willingness to use a female condom, and willingness to have an HIV test. The pilot concluded that:

> These differences in survey results can be largely attributed to the comprehensive approach to AIDS care, and critically to the inclusion of ARV treatment which has seen increase in uptake of VCT in the district from fewer than 1,000 HIV tests in 1998 to more than 12,000 in 2002. The number of HIV support groups has also increased dramatically; from 4 in 1998 to 23 in 2002. (WHO, 2003, p. 3)

Learning the Lessons

Many of the important lessons are contained in the foregoing but it is worthwhile identifying what seem to be the lessons that can with suitable modification be transferred elsewhere. These are as follows:

- The primary health care system can be mobilized to supply AIDS treatment within an integrated set of related services that includes VCT, treatment of OIs and psychosocial support.

- Treatment services can be decentralized down to the primary care level so as to ensure coverage and community involvement.
- Simple regimens with standardized clinical guidelines encourage adherence on the part of the patients and simplify the work of health professionals.
- Multidisciplinary teams including nurse-based care with a focus on psycho-social support provide for more effective use of resources and more holistic care.
- Comprehensive care that includes a wide range of support is essential for ensuring high levels of adherence to ART.
- A community-based programme of education about the value of ART is essential if people are to be informed about what constitutes effective use of ART, and is critical for increasing all aspects of understanding by communities of what constitutes a supportive environment for individuals and families.
- The cost of ARVs can be made more manageable through the use of generic drugs and through reductions in the cost of laboratory tests, so that many more people can afford ART.

The Khayelitsha programme is important precisely because of what it suggests about possible directions for the future in expanding access to ART. It suggests strongly that scaling up treatment is feasible and that this can be accomplished through a focus on expanding access to ARV and related services at the primary health care level. It has demonstrated that this is perfectly feasible, and that it is possible to achieve very favourable outcomes in terms of reduced morbidity and mortality, so that individuals, families and communities can manage the personal and social impact of HIV/AIDS.

The programme has demonstrated that all of these achievements are feasible within resource-constrained circumstances, and that, furthermore, there are measurable benefits in terms of strengthening activities and behaviours favourable to reducing HIV transmission. It has also demonstrated that prevention and care are indeed a continuum and that strengthening treatment is an effective route to better prevention outcomes. These are tremendous achievements, although MSF and others have warned that the challenges ahead remain considerable.

The programme has shown what is feasible for a relatively small peri-urban population in the richest country in Africa, but this does not necessarily provide a template that can be applied to the much poorer rural population of Africa. There is some limited evidence, however, that relates to pilot projects in a number of rural communities (Masaka in Uganda and KwaZulu-Natal in South Africa, for example) and these do support the proposition that ART is indeed feasible and can be provided without complex needs for health infrastructure.

What is clear from many projects is that affordability is an essential condition if poor people are to access ART, and that charging for VCT, laboratory tests and drugs will deter take-up of treatment. It follows that providing treatment for poor people will mean free provision and that even for the non-poor treatment will only be accessible for most people under highly subsidized conditions. Hence the need to ensure sustained funding for ART and related services for the foreseeable future in most countries if access is to be secured for the very large number of people who need it.

Where services have been provided under free or highly subsidized conditions, the level of adherence even among the poorest members of the community has been shown in many places to be as high as for other, better-off, groups. Poverty has thus not been a factor in determining successful outcomes with ART, but it is undeniably a factor which deters take-up where charges are applied for drugs and other services. Thus the Khayelitsha project had a positive bias towards the poor and yet this seems to have no measurably negative impact on the success of the programme.

Concluding Remarks

It is readily agreed by everyone that effective use of the additional financial resources that are now available is essential. In part this is because there are people in very large numbers who are desperately seeking treatment and in need of better care and support. Setting up systems and services to meet all these needs is the over-riding target. But perhaps just as important is the sustainability of service provision, and this will depend on demonstrating that resources have been effectively used. This follows in part from the dependence on international sources of funding (especially the Global Fund and MAP), and these flows will have to be maintained for many years to come.

If external resource flows are to be maintained, then it is critically important to be able to demonstrate that the funds have been effectively utilized. This means strengthening the capacity for improving service delivery not only in key areas such as VCT and MTCT, but also more generally in many other related areas. It cannot be said that so far enough resources and effort have been allocated to addressing capacity limitations of service development and service delivery. To a degree these limitations on performance are rectifiable, but there remain important constraints to scaling up services that are structural and deep-seated. Hence the call for comprehensive responses that begin to address the complexity of social, cultural and economic conditions.

Instead of the Millennium Development Goal target for 3 million people to be receiving ART by 2005, it looks more probable that the number will be less than one million. At the present time (May 2005) it is estimated by the WHO that about 4.1 million people in Africa have CD4 counts less than 200 and therefore in terms of the WHO guidelines require ART. But only 50,000 to 100,000 were estimated as receiving treatment in 2004, which is a mere 2 per cent of the total estimated by the WHO. It is possible to do better, much better, and much more is expected by those who are affected by HIV/AIDS in Africa.

To do better means identifying the constraints to programme development and service delivery; learning the lessons of how to scale up access to treatment; and moving forward with an integrated response that is genuinely inclusive of all stakeholders. The issues are not simply narrowly defined and technical but as much social and cultural, and need to be understood as such if there is to be rapid progress with widening access. It is absolutely essential that access to treatment be scaled up as a key priority in all countries, in part to reduce the morbidity and mortality caused by HIV/AIDS, and in part because the actual and potential socio-economic losses are so devastating for Africa.

The funds needed for an effective response to AIDS have been estimated by UNAIDS as $10.5 billion for 2005 rising to $15.5 in 2007 (from a level of $4.7 billion in 2003). These sums are well within the capacity of the donor community, private and public, and would have the added advantage for donors of offsetting levels of support in other areas, such as poverty alleviation programmes and emergency food supplies, while at the same time increasing the effectiveness of other expenditures (such as those needed to achieve Education for All [EFA] targets). In the aggregate the total benefits to African development from additional expenditures on AIDS activities have to be seen as generating high and positive returns.

If the MDG targets for poverty, educational access, HIV prevention, and so on, are to be attained, then human resources have to be sustained and to achieve this there has to be a rapid expansion of access to ARV treatment and improved levels of care and support. At this time it cannot be said that performance in any way matches needs, and the people of Africa will be the losers unless there are major initiatives specifically to improve policy and programme development and to widen access to services.

5
Community-Based Strategies: Lessons from Below

Introduction

For some time, it has been the position of many observers of this grotesquely perverse HIV/AIDS pandemic in Africa that community-based groups, not governmental strategies, have been the most effective means of engaging with the virus and its societal impacts. It is not difficult to see why: the central thrust of the information and education campaigns (IECs) has been to introduce norms and 'co-ordinate' messages. As a result, very large national programmes have been created in almost all countries on the continent to do nothing else. A central failing of this strategy has been the lack of action on social determinants of people in their groups and their societies: it is now well recognized that the decision to 'take action' is deeply influenced by social norms. In other words, people must want to protect themselves from infections, must know what their protection options are and must be able to practise them. In the case of African societies where polygamous and multi-partner relations are a significant part of the cultural norms (as detailed in chapter 2), IEC strategies demanded a radical change in these patterns of traditional behaviours without understanding their socio-cultural dynamics.

In contradistinction to the IEC strategy, community-based groups have succeeded because they have changed the emphasis from the content of the message to the characteristics of a community's organizations and institutions. As a result they have created strong community organizations that are dedicated to social equity, mutual caring and support, essential social services provision and community health promotion. However, the models of effectiveness, sustainability and local resource mobilization that those activities provide have yet to find their way into national or international HIV/AIDS or national development policies and strategies. Drawing on case studies, the central argument of this chapter is that intervention strategies need to be rooted in community responses, to understand both the impact of the epidemic and how to change their individual and organizational approaches to support community action.

Community Mitigation Efforts and Initiatives

The ability of households to manage the ill-health and death of one or more adult members depends on numerous factors: socio-economic status prior to the presence of HIV/AIDS; ability to minimize loss of assets and minimize debt; the support of extended family and of community and formal and informal support agencies. In addition, in many local communities, such as those in Zimbabwe, families affected by HIV/AIDS become subject to stigmatization and discrimination, leading to secrecy around the disease. These factors may be described in terms of stages in the sequence of impact and their reversibility. The impacts of the first stage include the reallocation of economic resources and labour. This impact may be temporary, and is reversible. The second stage is when family and household assets are sold to meet changed household needs. Children are deprived of education and care. This stage is difficult, if not impossible, to reverse. The household may then proceed to enter a stage of dependency on charity and aid, and/or eventually break up. This is the third and final stage of impacts. This model is likely to be too simplistic for programming purposes, but it does outline an initial method for a more thorough investigation of the patterns of impact. The lessons from the effectiveness of existing programme designs help fill in some of the outstanding questions about responding to the social and economic needs of HIV/AIDS-affected families and communities.

Turning to the secrecy resulting from stigma and discrimination, a South African survey, based on focus group discussions with people living with HIV/AIDS, reported that the negative orientation to people with HIV/AIDS, even when only exhibited by a minority of community members, and the fear of negative reactions from community members and other persons, is sufficiently strong to provide reason for PLWHA not to be open about their status in their own communities. PLWHA described how they had found it much easier to talk about their HIV positive status in other communities and only later within their own community. Interestingly, support networks did not seem to have evolved, and the individuals living with HIV felt very alone in their struggle to lead positive lives. Social support networks are important for well-being, and so the building of a strong support base for PLWHA is a priority.

The same survey found that, as of 2001, little community mobilization in South Africa had occurred around HIV/AIDS issues, other than information campaigns run from outside communities. This seems in line with findings in Zimbabwe, where affected households report often turning to extended family and/or community members for help. A study found that about half of affected households studied in urban and rural areas of Zimbabwe had asked for some help with food or money from relatives, friends and neighbours within the previous twelve months (Kaliyati et al., 2003). One of the greatest needs was money for school fees. However, those same families reported that the help they needed often was not forthcoming.

Thus, any discussion about community mobilization should understand and include the need to thoroughly describe the context, given the marked differentiation in forms, intensity, duration and levels of community mobilization to address various issues arising from HIV/AIDS. While a number of effective initiatives can be cited (see below), in other instances relatively little is being done by and with communities. For example, in the Eastern Cape of South Africa, only 27 per cent of adults report ever having been to a meeting of people where AIDS had been discussed (Centre for AIDS Development, Research and Evaluation-Cadre, 2002). This supports the impression that there is very little community-level mobilization around HIV/AIDS issues. Additionally, there is little evidence that structures for prevention, care or support are emerging. There is a need for access to advice, information and support at village level, including remote villages with little access to services.

Although institutional support seems a critical factor in assisting households, some communities do provide support for affected households without external interventions. UNAIDS (1999) outlines four forms of community-based responses to HIV/AIDS:

- social support groups, including labour sharing, grain savings and food donations;
- savings associations;
- emergency assistance associations, including interventions by faith-based groups; and
- self-help groups of people with HIV/AIDS.

All of these are little understood in the context of addressing the impact of HIV/AIDS. Whether these local, informal and sometimes spontaneous responses can be strengthened from outside is unclear. Imposing external views and expectations may undermine local initiatives and ownership. Poorly designed and externally imposed programmes could also jeopardize fledgeling community initiatives.

In addition, while the strengths and capacity of local communities are often credited as a substantive means to cope with the multiple impacts of HIV/AIDS, there are limits imposed by the wider economic context. A study of both urban and rural locales in Zimbabwe found that the difficult economic conditions facing most people prevented communities from offering any or much assistance. While a grain savings scheme was highlighted for its effectiveness in providing for some of the needs of rural people, churches, savings clubs and other informal support networks offered only limited assistance to affected households. This, too, is likely due to the constraints imposed by the general economy. Evidence from Kenya, Tanzania and Uganda indicates active concern by such networks, but the demand far exceeds any one organization's ability to respond fully. The ability and willingness of communities to assist households affected by HIV/AIDS vary greatly within and across countries. In many cases, communities would be willing to do more, but lack the resources.

Thus, outside assistance is likely to be essential, or at least be an option, for communities to access. Furthermore, while the above examples illustrate that the responses of communities can be negative, one feature in these examples is the absence of positive images and directions that can alter the negative images and response. An outside organization or firm local leadership may provide an alternative framework to the fear and stigma that may exist. There are some well-studied programmes that offer credible and effective models for working with communities. In cases where sensitive programmes, often led by NGOs with long-established community presence, have implemented flexible responses, the results reflect support that serves people's needs. Four of those NGO-supported programmes are outlined below.

Families, Orphans and Children Under Stress (FOCUS) is a programme of FACT, a Zimbabwean AIDS service organization established in 1987. It is an example of how local ownership and commitment combined with very modest outside economic assistance can succeed in mounting a comprehensive programme on HIV/AIDS. It is centred in eastern Zimbabwe and uses churches as a basis for its outreach to affected families and communities. Its purpose is to provide care and support to orphaned children. The programme relies on community volunteers, usually women. It emphasizes identification and monitoring of vulnerable children through visiting households regularly, providing community ownership, keeping children in school, establishing income-generating activities, and training and motivating volunteers. Volunteers identify unmet basic household needs and provide essential material support, including maize seed, fertilizer, food, clothing, blankets and school fees. The visiting volunteers also offer emotional and spiritual support to the children and their caregivers. In 2000, over 2,700 orphaned children were registered and supported by nearly 180 active volunteers. The total programme cost was $20,000–30,000 per year, a very reasonable sum.

The Community-Oriented Primary Education (COPE) Programme in Malawi, operated by Save the Children (US), is an example where initial outside assistance has facilitated a thriving local response. The programme mobilized communities at area and village levels to address the needs of orphaned and other vulnerable children. In addition to community participants, government, religious and business groups were involved. With the facilitation of COPE programme staff, area villagers came together to assess their concerns. The number of COPE staff was eventually reduced substantially as village and area AIDS committees assumed greater control and ownership over the functioning of activities. The local committees were linked to government and religious services, creating a stronger network of support in the process. By 2000, over 200 village AIDS committees existed. Over 12,000 orphaned children and nearly 12,000 families had received food and other material assistance. The average annual cost was $317,000.

Chikankata is a mission-run health facility in southern Zambia. Over a period of ten years an HIV/AIDS programme has evolved that is based on basic community development principles: strong local ownership and direction, building on the skills and knowledge of a wide range of people and groups, supplementing local resources with external aid. Initially, the medical staff of Chikankata sought to provide treatment for people living with HIV/AIDS through mobile clinics. This proved to be too costly and insufficient to meet people's daily needs. Over time, the programme moved into family training for home-based care and then into mobilizing communities to be involved in care of people with HIV/AIDS. As community members confronted the needs of affected families, they designed initiatives that drew upon the resources of local government departments and organizations. The approach that has evolved at Chikankata has, like the FOCUS and COPE programmes, become a model for other eastern and southern African groups.

A programme in Luweero District, Uganda, illustrates the power of simple organization and local ownership. The programme is run by the African Medical & Research Foundation (AMREF) and Lutheran World Relief and is designed to address the range of needs of affected individuals and families. It encompasses a variety of support functions, from assisting with school fees for orphaned and other vulnerable children, to developing water supplies, to micro-finance loans for business activities. A three-tier structure has been created to respond to problems, including the large number of orphaned children in the area. Organizationally, guardians of orphaned children are linked to Village Orphan Committees and select their representatives on those committees. Guardians may be grandparents, older siblings, aunts or uncles, or non-relatives. The Village Orphan Committees maintain a register of vulnerable children and help generate local resources to support the children and their guardians. In turn, the committees select representatives to Parish Orphan Committees and these are linked to local government authorities. A sense of local ownership is strong at all these levels and the committees have begun tackling other development problems. Community members have seen notable changes in the well-being of children and affected families.

Case Study I:
Youth Net and Counselling (YONECO)

A good example of a community-based organization is the Youth Net and Counselling (YONECO) organization in Zomba, Malawi. Zomba is located in the Southern Region, 65 km from Blantyre. The HIV prevalence in Zomba is not known, but it is generally believed to be at least as high as in Blantyre, that is, in the range of 25 to 30 per cent among the 15- to 49-year age group. In 1997, the Domasi College of Education in Zomba disbanded its intra-mural HIV prevention programme because of lack of funding. A group of lecturers involved in the programme decided to continue the work, however, and with the assistance of local churches and the participation of young people from Zomba they formed YONECO. The organization moved from the college premises to a small room in town, and for a period of about two years it conducted public awareness and public education activities for HIV prevention on a volunteer basis without any external funding.

In September 1999, YONECO received a capacity building grant from an international programme dedicated to building community HIV competence. This allowed the organization to move to more accessible and functional premises, and to employ some essential administrative and programme staff. Almost immediately YONECO underwent a transformation from an informal group of volunteers who were only visible when they staged or participated in public events, into a widely known and respected community institution that was solicited to provide services. The local school boards approached YONECO with the request to revive the school peer education anti-AIDS clubs that had been set up some years before with international funding but that had since become dormant.

By early 2001, YONECO worked in four of the local School Zones of the Ministry of Education, each with an average of sixteen primary and secondary schools. YONECO had trained two to four peer educators in each school and regularly monitored, supervised and supported the activities of the anti-AIDS clubs in these institutions. Through its activities of organizing clubs for out-of-school children, YONECO became aware that many children who were at highest risk of HIV infection were the children of sex workers who plied their trade on the periphery of the large police and army barracks in and around Zomba. This led to the development of a peer support and education programme for sex workers. By April 2001, the programme included sixty active sex workers and distributed between 15,000 and 20,000 condoms monthly.

Meanwhile, YONECO had attracted the attention of other funding agencies and had received funds from several different sources. This allowed it to move to even larger premises and greatly to expand its programme of activities to include prevention of drug abuse, environmental programming, home care, counselling and income-generating activities for people living with HIV. Lately, YONECO has started to work with traditional authorities involved in the very secretive and prolonged sexual initiation and circumcision rites of the Yao people. The rites involve, in some instances, sexual initiation of very young girls by adult males, a practice that only recently has been considered to constitute sexual abuse of children. At the same time, the rites are a potential opportunity to introduce sexual health and gender education to young boys undergoing circumcision and girls undergoing training for womanhood.

Just two years after receiving a very modest capacity development grant, YONECO has grown from a small barely known group of volunteers with no organizational budget into the primary AIDS service organization in Zomba with an annual budget of about $200,000. YONECO is now known everywhere in town. The grounds of the YONECO offices are a popular meeting place for young people. The organization receives numerous requests from schools, companies, local government, churches and traditional leaders to help start programmes in response to AIDS.

The growth of YONECO is an example of the catalytic effect of providing organizational support rather than activity support to emerging community-based organizations. It also demonstrates how programmes tend to develop and expand in scope when they are being driven by community needs and demands rather than by national frameworks or external donor policies. Finally, YONECO demonstrates the concept of community HIV competence. The community of Zomba has gained in HIV competence because of the growth of YONECO within its confines. There now is a local AIDS service organization that is well known and has a widely acknowledged presence where formerly there was none.

Although a description of the community of Zomba before and after the creation of YONECO provides plausible evidence for the benefit, the question still remains what level of proof is required to be certain that the community's susceptibility to HIV and vulnerability to AIDS has really changed. The model needs validation, and the result of this validation will depend to a large extent on the mode and method of inquiry. It is also important to note that the types of activities carried out by the members and staff of YONECO are not unique or unusual. Peer education in schools, peer action programmes among female sex workers, condom promotion, home care, self-help groups of people living with HIV, working with traditional circumcisers – these are all recognized initiatives for HIV prevention and AIDS care. The difference, however, is that these are not projects that have been imported into Zomba as part of a national strategy or an international project. Each one of these activities started in response to a felt community need, and before any external funding for the activity became available.

Case Study II: The National Community of Women Living with HIV/AIDS (NACWOLA)

The National Community of Women Living with HIV/AIDS (NACWOLA) in Uganda has done exemplary work in providing sustained and transformative care and support services for women living with or affected by HIV/AIDS (see box 5.1). As a community-based organization, NACWOLA, like The AIDS Support Organization (TASO), has a long experience behind it in devising ways of reducing the vulnerability of PLWHA. It works towards spiritual support, stigma management and boosting self-dignity.

One of the most successful projects of NACWOLA is the so-called 'Memory Project'. The Memory Project at NACWOLA has been so successful that many other countries have adopted it. The project basically consists of training sessions of HIV-positive parents to enable them to communicate better with their children through developing a memory book (Callinan, 2000). In the memory book, parents are able to disclose their sero-status and all health issues to their children in comfortable ways. The book also helps such parents to plan for their children's future by establishing guardianship arrangements as well as recording important family history and precious memories. The main goal of the project is to assist HIV-positive parents in providing their children with the support they need to survive with as little trauma as possible after their parents have died. In so doing, the infected parent copes better with the disease, death and grief. The writing process strengthens mutual communication between parent and children about extremely difficult issues.

NACWOLA members testified to the usefulness of the Memory Project, reporting that it enhanced children's involvement in their coping with HIV/AIDS. They also said that the project worked to reduce the stress, anxiety and guilt and the burdens of secrecy. For all of them, it helped them

Box 5.1 National Community of Women Living with
HIV/AIDS (NACWOLA)

NACWOLA is a unique organization in that it is exclusively run by and for Ugandan women living with HIV/AIDS. Membership presently stands at 40,000 with twenty-three branches nationwide. Founded in 1992, its mission is to improve the quality of life of women living with HIV/AIDS and their families.

The objectives of the organization include to:

- fight stigma and abuse directed towards HIV/AIDS-positive women and their families;
- access and impart information on HIV/AIDS to members;
- economically empower its members so as to reduce vulnerability and dependency;
- unite all women living with HIV/AIDS for psycho-social support and to speak with one voice;
- equip members and their families with coping mechanisms; and
- contribute to the prevention campaign through advocacy.

Other activities of NACWOLA include:

- its newsletter, *Positive Woman*, which is published in six Ugandan languages and focuses on gender-related issues for women living with HIV/AIDS;
- legal services which it provides to its members in collaboration with the International Federation of Women Lawyers (FIDA) Uganda in the areas of property grabbing, inheritance, domestic violence, will writing, marriage, divorce, etc.; and
- a very successful 'Memory Project' (see text).

cope better with worries about their children's future and to confront their own deaths psychologically. Today, the Memory Project has spread to TASO members and other community centres throughout the country as a collective responsibility for children's guidance (Kaleeba, 2001; Nabwire, 2000).

Furthermore, through community-based outreach programmes, NACWOLA provides counselling services. Field visits are arranged whereby members who have been training as counsellors regularly go to the homes of PLWHA to offer palliative care, psychological counselling and spiritual comfort. Care is taken to peer-match so that clients are paired with counsellors who have similar backgrounds, particularly regarding age and sex. Older PLWHA, for example, are extremely uncomfortable discussing their intimate sexual lives or their bodies with counsellors who are young enough to be their children. Another grassroots intervention undertaken by NACWOLA to alleviate the effects of HIV/AIDS-related stigma and discrimination is the hiring of the services of a lawyer to deal with legal issues connected with discrimination, property grabbing and will writing. The organization takes care of the lawyer's retainer fees and s/he provides these services to members free of charge.

Case Study III: The Health Rights Action Group (HAG)

By the nature of its work, Uganda's Health Rights Action Group (HAG) collaborates with and partners a lot of other local groups that work in the area of health rights (box 5.2). For example, in 2002 it joined the Coalition for Health Promotion and Social Development (HEPS) to challenge a move by the Uganda Law Reform Commission to complete a draft bill on intellectual property rights. They appealed for more time to raise awareness and allow for proper discussion of the bill by the public. HEPS wanted to ensure that the law does not pave the way for patent holders to short-change

---

Box 5.2 The Health Rights Action Group (HAG)

HAG was established in 2001 with a mission to provide a forum to advocate for health rights, care, management and treatment for HIV/AIDS and other diseases.
  Its objectives include:

- the mobilization and sensitizing of communities about access to treatment, care, management and support of HIV/AIDS and other diseases;
- the protection of legal, ethical and social rights of PLWHA;
- advocacy of and support for the development of policies and equitable laws on procurement of pharmaceuticals, including generic drugs;
- support and promotion of the development of information, education and communication materials on health issues for use in educational institutions and in communities;
- advocacy for the rights of women, children and other vulnerable groups; and
- empowerment of PLWHA to live positively and support their survival skills.

Other activities include the following:

- In partnership with Physicians for Human Rights, a US-based NGO, HAG runs workshops to sensitize health professionals on the rights of PLWHA.
- HAG runs a programme called 'Women Treatment Action' in nine districts. It is dedicated to activities to increase access to essential medication for HIV/AIDS and related ailments for women and girls.
- The groundbreaking study that HAG conducted in 2002 on the status of human rights among Ugandan PLWHA revealed: 'human rights concerns for PLWHA still pose a big challenge to the nation'.

Ugandans by setting unrealistic prices for AIDS drugs. More recently, HEPS formed a sub-group known as the 'Uganda Coalition for Access to Essential Medicines' with the objective of advocating for fair legislation and access to essential drugs.

In dealing with the stigma and discrimination that PLWHA suffer at the workplace, HAG employs a full-time legal and human rights officer. At the time of writing, they were handling two big cases and had just secured an out of court settlement for another client. The latter had been unjustly dismissed by his employers – a religious-based organization – on account of his HIV/AIDS status, despite the fact that he had produced a doctor's report that clearly stated that he was fit to fulfil his work duties. The second, pending case involves a female worker who, ironically, was formerly employed by a human rights body in Kampala. She alleges that she was unjustly dismissed from work primarily because of the fact that she is a PLWHA. Investigations in this case were still underway at the time of writing.

Community advocacy for action on stigma and HIV/AIDS spearheaded by NGOs like HAG is partly responsible for the new trend whereby private sector businesses are getting involved in addressing issues of AIDS-related stigma and discrimination. Of course it also makes good business sense for the human resources departments of private companies and big corporations to respond positively to the epidemic. By implementing HIV/AIDS programmes and policies, companies avoid a loss of productivity and profits due to the illness of their workers, increased labour costs occasioned by absenteeism, a loss of skills and experience as illness forces workers to quit their jobs, and the overall threats that the pandemic poses to markets and the economies in which they operate. Hence, several companies within the Ugandan private sector have recently launched HIV/AIDS programmes that aim not only to educate employees about HIV/AIDS, but also to pay for ARV treatment to infected workers (at times including their immediate families). Most of the companies that have developed such policies are multinational corporations such

as Shell (Uganda), Coca Cola, British American Tobacco
(BAT), Celtel, MTN, Nile Breweries, Unilever and Standard
Chartered Bank. However, the process of developing these
policies is not always participatory. As Milly Katana, the
HAG lobbying and advocacy officer, said, 'For these policies
to work, they must be people-based. HIV is about people;
therefore, the way they live, relate, talk, must be integrated
into the implementation of these policies.' Government
as well as local companies and manufacturers are yet to
catch up.

Lesson Learned from the Communities

These and other examples of NGO-supported local programmes illustrate some of the key components of effective
responses to the impact of HIV/AIDS:

- strong local ownership and control over decision making;
- the evolution of programmes over time, allowing for
  experiences to inform decisions;
- facilitation, not control, from outside, especially with volunteers, and recognition of established or new leadership;
  and
- functional links to all levels of community resources,
  including government social services.

These examples reflect an integrated community response to
HIV/AIDS. They are integrated in being able to draw upon
the resources and skills of all community groups and agencies, not simply a health clinic or school. They are also considered integrated in that they address the underlying causes
of issues, including the reasons for poverty and political
disenfranchisement. There are variations on the models,
some with a formal centre from which the activities are co-
ordinated and others more loosely organized. Some programmes use only a portion of the integrated community
models. For example, many home-based care programmes in

southern Africa are designed to offer a continuum of care, especially palliative care, for PLWHA. Often support for family members is included. A programme may be structured around a care centre or similar, located within the community, possibly attached to a church or school, from where home-based care services are co-ordinated. Volunteers, supported by medical and community development staff, play a major role in the functioning of this model.

Some NGO programmes offer only specific services. For example, they may provide assistance to individuals and families in preparing for death and its consequences. This preparation may involve the making of individual memory books by ill parents that will be passed along to children, or the drafting of wills to formalize and legalize asset transfers. Such services may also be a part of a wider programme for PLWHA and affected families.

A good deal of emphasis has been placed on increasing the economic well-being of affected households and of HIV-infected individuals. This has taken several forms: education grants for school children, food relief, and small loans/grants for what are generically called income-generating activities (IGAs). Many of these programmes arise from experiences over the past two decades with micro-finance to stimulate small business formation and economic security for groups of women and men. Although there is much enthusiasm for IGAs among NGOs dealing with HIV/AIDS in communities, implementation and sustainability remain to be fully assessed. To date, experiences with IGA loans and grants have had a very mixed record, with the trend being towards initiatives that are non-sustainable in the absence of fairly substantial (by local standards) outside organizational support, or that are of such a small scale as to offer little economic value to all but a handful of individuals.

More effective are initiatives that have addressed the poverty underlying HIV/AIDS through established micro-finance agencies. The experience of working with micro-finance programmes and recipients, as opposed to simply setting up income-generating activities with small grants, provides improved design and structures, greater sophistication in offering finance for a range of needs and uses, and usually involves facilitation for expanding community mobilization. Several programmes in Uganda and Zambia have been identified as exhibiting 'best practices'. In Uganda, these include a programme supported by the Foundation for International Community Assistance (FINCA) that offers loans for family health and funeral insurance and community mitigation efforts and the programme discussed earlier in this chapter supported by AMREF/Lutheran World Relief to provide loans for business support and a strong community mobilization component. In Zambia, the SCOPE project has been identified for the effectiveness of its loans to communities to develop mitigation activities. There remains, however, a need for more descriptive experiences with and critical analyses of micro-financing activities for HIV/AIDS prevention and mitigation, especially initiatives that engage communities.

Faith-Based Initiatives

Many faith-based groups are playing a significant role around HIV/AIDS issues. For example, two of the examples cited above of community mobilization are associated with faith-based support and involvement (FOCUS in Zimbabwe and Chikankata in Zambia). Congregations are involved in care and support for PLWHA, affected families and orphaned children. Home visits and spiritual support by congregation members are common. Different activities are stressed according to the policies and traditions of various faith-based groups: for example, the Catholic Church in many areas provides support for affected households and for orphaned children, whereas the Evangelical Lutheran Church in Tanzania runs health facilities and provides medical attention.

Many faith-based responses go unreported, in part because secular NGOs and international agencies have been cautious, if not sceptical, about the commitment of faith groups to address HIV/AIDS prevention. To a significant extent this scepticism is fuelled by the opposition of some faith-based groups, notably the Catholic Church, to the promotion and use of condoms. This anti-condom position shows no sign of abating under Pope Benedict XVI. Nor have faith groups done a good job of publicizing their positive contributions. The lack of good documentation on the roles and contributions of faith groups remains a major gap in organizing and promoting society-wide responses to HIV/AIDS.

What is clear is that many local faith communities are highly concerned and actively involved in HIV/AIDS issues. Church and mosque members provide spiritual, emotional and material support to affected households, contribute to the support of orphaned children, and take a lead in organizing other community members to mitigate the impact of HIV/AIDS. Denominations as a whole, however, have been slow to speak out on HIV/AIDS issues, invest substantial resources or offer sustained leadership. This has made the work of local faith groups more difficult and isolated.

Concluding Remarks

The most striking feature about the HIV epidemic is that individuals and communities have been mobilized and empowered by it. To date, many NGOs, CBOs, FBOs and other organizations, including those run by people living with HIV/AIDS, have developed extensive skills and experience in working with their constituents. People are speaking out; community groups are coming into existence. As the examples in this chapter show, the experience of successful HIV prevention, treatment and care programmes, as well as humanitarian relief and welfare activities such as caring for children orphaned by AIDS, has demonstrated again and again the importance of community involvement and social mobilization against the epidemic. However, many governments have been reluctant fully to acknowledge or support the contributions of civil society groups. There seems to be a fear among government staff that their technical and administrative authority will be over-shadowed by local organizations. Other government authorities worry that some civil society groups are overly critical and threaten existing political legitimacy.

Those concerns within government are not trivial, but in the context of HIV/AIDS they are slowing effective responses. What is needed is a new form of partnership, a partnership which places people at the centre of the response to the epidemic. This will enable the activities of government to reflect and build upon the complex nature of people's daily lives and to address their needs in a cohesive manner. It will begin the process of breaking down a compartmentalized development approach to essentially interlinked conditions – poverty, disempowerment, disease, subordination, illiteracy, land ownership, to mention a few – and HIV infection. Under this partnership, governments will recognize and accept that little is simple in the face of this epidemic and in so doing will provide the basis for hope and belief that we are not powerless in the face of this pathogen and that we will indeed overcome the epidemic and its consequences.

6
Setting Priorities for Confronting HIV/AIDS in Africa

Introduction

If we accept without qualification that an estimated 20 million people have died since the start of the HIV/AIDS epidemic in Africa and that a further 25.2 million are presently living with the virus on the continent, then it is reasonable to assume that by 2015 more than 45 million people will have died from HIV-related illnesses. If it is further assumed, conservatively, that only five people within the immediate family are affected for every person who dies, then some 200 million people are closely affected. To this number need to be added those less directly affected in extended families, colleagues at work, close friends in faith and other communities – perhaps a doubling of those directly affected to give a total of some 400 million at the lowest estimate.

What is demonstrated by such crude calculations is that the scale of the impact of the epidemic in Africa is such that most of the population is affected by what is happening. The epidemic has effects on social, political and economic life that we have not witnessed previously, such that all development activities, including those relating to security at national, regional and international levels, have to explicitly address the implications of what is evolving as a huge humanitarian disaster: the epidemic undermines development and thus further worsens the conditions in which HIV transmission thrives, simultaneously reducing the capacity of families, communities and nations to cope with the complex social, political and economic consequences.

Furthermore, it poses with increasing immediacy the additional challenge of how the transitions towards democratic governance in Africa can remain on track amid prevalence levels of HIV/AIDS as high as 10, 20, 30 and 40 percent of the adult population, in some African countries. Though the exact mechanisms through which the epidemic affects state–society relations are not fully mapped, and, as a result, poorly understood, emerging evidence from high-prevalence countries indicates that the impact could be quite severe. It is further exaggerated by existing weaknesses in governance systems, such as reforms of the civil services, staff departures to the private sector or other countries, and financial constraints undertaken at the behest of international agencies. At the same time, these other changes mask the true impacts of HIV/AIDS and slow effective responses.

Will the broader international community provide the resources in the volumes required to enable these nations to continue to function? Will there be global social safety nets to allow the survival of nations rendered poor by this epidemic, and the poor within nations? Will governments on the African continent maintain the leadership required to overcome the crisis? In what follows, I will examine some of the main challenges that policy makers need to overcome in order to prevent further spread of the epidemic, as well as mitigate the impact it has and will continue to have on the continent.

The Four Core Imperatives

HIV/AIDS is compromising the ability of government agencies to deliver the goods and services expected of them. As employees become ill and leave government services, their skills, training and acquired knowledge are lost. Existing service delivery constraints are further affected, with multi-dimensional productivity and efficiency impacts across all government agencies, private sector businesses and civil society groups. The cumulative impacts of HIV/AIDS are already costly for nations and families – and will become more so without active interventions. As production and service delivery are disrupted, income is likely to fall. Families and businesses shift spending from productive activities to medical care and related benefits, with less going to savings, productive activities and government revenues. At the same time, the costs associated with dealing with the epidemic increase – for governments, businesses of all sizes and individuals and families.

The HIV/AIDS epidemic is not uniform in its impacts; not all groups of people are equally affected. Young people, many already without hope for economic security, face an even bleaker future. Women, many already living in poverty, are vulnerable to the loss of income and family labour. Extended family and community support systems are stressed to provide assistance as they would have in the past. Sections of the rural economy are producing less food and income, not only for local needs but for the nation as a whole. The epidemic puts at risk education, health and other development achievements of recent decades. National commitments to reduce poverty and socio-economic and gender inequalities are becoming more difficult to achieve.

As the impact of HIV/AIDS runs its course over the next two decades, the key issue is how to maintain and expand the ability of the state to supply essential goods and services that affect all sectors of society. One of the biggest political challenges will be to prevent the hollowing out of state structures because of staff losses and reduced resources. It will require minimizing the current and future losses of human resources, especially in key development sectors. It will require new approaches to supporting both rural and urban livelihoods.

To meet these challenges, policy makers will need to confront and overcome the following core imperatives: the imperative of an *effective* response; the imperative of a *co-ordinated* response; the imperative of a *sustainable* response; and the imperative of *working with local communities*.

A prerequisite of an effective response is a common understanding of the nature of the epidemic, which takes into account the long-term nature of its impacts. This we do not yet have. This should not surprise us for the epidemic is a new and complex phenomenon for which there is no likeness in living memory, not one drawn from war, from disease, from natural disasters or from man-made ones. This is not to say that we are blindly groping. We are doing what we know needs to be done (behaviour modification strategies) while we search for new and more effective ways to respond. The more we share a vision of an effective way forward, the more co-ordination and the building of partnerships will naturally follow.

The second imperative, that of a co-ordinated response, means that we must build the partnerships required to ensure that the search for effective sustainable policies and interventions is an ongoing process and that duplication and strategic impediments to development are minimized. This has three components. First, there needs to be a greater harmonization of policies between donor governments, multilateral institutions of global economic governance and African countries. This will ensure that the fight against HIV/AIDS does not destabilize or impinge on longer-term economic and development strategies. Second, greater partnerships are needed between NGOs and community groups responding to the pandemic, on the one hand, and national governments, on the other. This will ensure that the needs and knowledge accumulated by groups at the sharp end of service delivery and care support are reflected in national strategic plans for confronting HIV/AIDS. Finally, there needs to be greater co-ordination of the efforts of multilateral agencies (particularly the UN system) within African countries. This will minimize duplication of efforts while ensuring that available resources are better utilized.

The third imperative is that of a sustainable response. New programmes of support, funded increasingly by the Global Fund, the World Bank, private foundations, corporations, bilateral donors and national governments, have transformed the opportunities for developing and implementing effective responses to the HIV epidemic in Africa. But major challenges remain. For example, despite the recent increase in financial support for African governments in their response to HIV/AIDS, at the present time the various funding sources are only a fraction of what is needed and it is doubtful if their longer-term sustainability is assured. What, for example, will happen to the programmes currently being funded by the Global Fund, when that organization – as is expected – comes to the end of its five-year mandate in 2007? Similarly, how will governments currently providing treatment and care for people living with HIV/AIDS be able to maintain these critical life-sustaining services once the available extra-budgetary funds from donor governments are utilized?

The final imperative is that of working with and learning from local communities. The commitment and contributions of affected individuals and communities have yet to be recognized or valued but they are extensive. They lie at the heart of a sustainable response to this epidemic but in most cases they need to be supplemented by further human and financial resources. The closeness of these individuals and communities to the problems and needs created by the epidemic generally ensures that they know best what are appropriate responses. However, these responses must also be ranked in order of effectiveness since resources, whether of individuals, communities, nations or external support agencies, will continue to be limited and will themselves be reduced by the epidemic.

Strategic Opportunities and Challenges

In addition to the core imperatives noted above, policy makers face a number of critical opportunities as well as challenges as they seek effective solutions to overcoming the epidemic. In what follows, I will group the main challenges and opportunities under the following four broad headings: greater leadership; sustained funding; effective prevention strategies; and effective treatment provision.

Greater Leadership

Opportunities A watershed was reached with the adoption in 2001, by Africa's heads of States and Government, of the Abuja Declaration on HIV/AIDS, tuberculosis and other related infectious diseases, as well as the 2001 UNGASS Declaration of Commitment. Through these and other declarations, African governments vigorously committed themselves to curbing the spread and mitigating the impact of the epidemic. As stated in Abuja, 'strong leadership at all levels of society is essential for an effective response to the epidemic'. Taking action on these declarations, most African countries have adopted national mechanisms for co-ordination and acceleration of the response to AIDS, such as national strategic AIDS plans, and high-level HIV/AIDS commissions and co-ordinating bodies. Parallel to this process, countries are taking opportunity of international funds available for treatment and other crucial areas in the response to HIV.

Challenges A major challenge for African leaders remains to mobilize societies and guide national and international action towards translating these commitments into results on the ground. Harnessing leadership at the personal, community and international levels, be it in a formal (political or bureaucratic) or informal (cultural leaders, household heads) form, is absolutely necessary to contain the epidemic. In particular, governments and state leaders have the prime responsibility and moral authority for initiating and promoting the necessary changes to tackle the epidemic. Much more still needs to be done in promoting legislation, executing policies and allocating resources.

There are a number of actions that African governments can and should take as a matter of urgency, and that only to a limited extent depend on increased funding or capacity. First, countries can ensure that HIV/AIDS-related concerns are included consistently across all sectoral policies, not just those related to health. This could for example mean addressing HIV/AIDS-related challenges to maintaining agricultural output. Second, budget priorities should reflect stated concern about HIV/AIDS. Heeding the commitment from Abuja, to allocate 15 per cent of the health budget to HIV/AIDS would significantly increase resources available for the fight against the epidemic in most African countries. Third, legislators should ensure both that the country's legislation is in harmony with HIV/AIDS-related pledges and commitments entered into, and that the legislation protects those infected and affected by HIV/AIDS.

Policies to ensure that human capacity is sustained and increased are key to mitigating the effect of the epidemic as demand for services increases, but the workforce dwindles. This is the case across all sectors. However, governments particularly need to focus on alternative solutions to increasing capacity for scaling up health sector responses, such as increasing provision of treatment and care and ensuring more effective partnership between public, private and faith-based health services provision. Such solutions could entail revising qualification requirements (shortening duration of training of health care workers in order to train more) and devising strategies for retention of staff and public provision of resources to private and faith-based health care institutions.

In relation to external partners, the number of funding institutions and partners is growing. This raises the challenge of effectively co-ordinating and channelling all programmes through the national strategic plans and institutions. It is necessary to strengthen the capacity and authority of national institutions to ensure the most effective use of increasing funding in supporting national processes and avoiding duplication of actions. The overwhelming demands placed on countries by different donors and partners have recently been addressed by the introduction of the principle of the 'Three Ones': one agreed Action Framework that provides the basis for co-ordination; one National Co-ordinating Authority with a broad-based mandate; and one agreed country-level monitoring and evaluation system (UNAIDS et al., 2004).

Increased Funding for AIDS

Opportunities The global community, recognizing the magnitude of the HIV/AIDS epidemic and its devastating effects on the African continent, is increasingly making resources available for the fight against HIV/AIDS in Africa. Available funding has increased from around $300 million in low- and middle- income countries in 1996, to an estimated $6.7 billion in 2005. Four main funding streams support AIDS programmes: domestic spending, bilateral assistance, multilateral agencies and the private sector. It is projected that bilateral assistance will grow faster in the near future, primarily as a result of the implementation of the US President's $15 billion 'President's Emergency Plan for AIDS Relief' (PEPFAR).

A number of countries have significantly increased their spending on HIV/AIDS, and domestic spending, including public as well as individual spending, accounts for about half of the spending on the epidemic (UNAIDS Global Resource Tracking Consortium, 2004). In addition, an array of international initiatives provide funds for HIV/AIDS-related work. For example, the Global Fund disbursed its first round of funds in 2002. Countries have also used the Global Fund for activities to attain goals set under the WHO's '3 by 5' initiative: an ambitious initiative to provide HIV/AIDS-related treatment to 3 million people in developing countries by 2005.

Challenges Although the funding available for HIV/AIDS responses has increased substantially, the need far outstrips the available resources. At the time of writing, in 2005, the estimated annual need for an adequate global response is $12 billion, increasing to $20 billion by 2007. Annual total AIDS spending, however, will likely increase from $4.7 billion in 2003 to only $10 billion in 2007, and the gap between need and available resources will increase unless new resources are brought in (UNAIDS Global Resource Tracking Consortium, 2004). The Global Fund is seriously underfunded. The pledges for contributions to the Fund so far total about $6.1 billion while only just under $3.7 billion has actually been received.[1]

Some countries have 'ceilings' on public spending, imposed by international financial institutions such as the IMF, put in place to ensure macro-economic stability. However, these ceilings have meant that countries have been unable to channel external, additional funding for AIDS through public budgets, and therefore have been unable to receive this funding altogether. A dialogue between countries and the IMF is taking place to resolve this dilemma, but so far it has not been resolved.

An increasing concern is that the funding that is available is to a large extent earmarked for purposes that may or may not be in tune with national AIDS response priorities. For example, the bulk of the available funding, such as that available through the Global Fund, is earmarked for drugs, while the country may prioritize (and also need) health care personnel training or in other ways need to increase the capacity of the health care system. Within funding for drug procurement, a challenge is that some funds may be earmarked for certain types of drugs. PEPFAR funding, for example, can only be spent on drugs approved by the US Food and Drug Administration. This translates into brand-name, more expensive drugs than generics, disbursed by other initiatives. In the same country, it is therefore possible to find different initiatives disbursing treatment according to different treatment protocols. When the funding dries up, the Ministry of Health will have to sustain these different regimes, an almost impossible task in countries with weak health infrastructures – infrastructures that the same funding cannot be used to strengthen.

Effective Prevention Strategies

Opportunities Although not enough is known about the epidemic, two decades of prevention and mitigation activities have provided an understanding of the dynamics of its spread, as well as its impact from the individual, via the household to the community and structural levels. The African experience has shown that the earlier focus on individual behaviour change is inadequate in the context of poverty and gender discrimination. Presently, successful programmes focus on the individual in the wider context of family, community and society, and on providing the right economic and other frameworks to empower individuals to take responsibility for themselves and those around them. Increasing availability of HIV/AIDS-related treatment necessitates working with communities to increase the uptake of these services, in turn opening new inroads to individuals and communities for prevention activities.

Challenges Prevention of further spread of the epidemic is still the cornerstone of HIV/AIDS-related efforts in Africa. Experience demonstrates that for prevention to be successful, it must be an integrated, communal effort. This means that a prerequisite of change at the individual level is a change at the level of societal structure and set of beliefs and traditions. For example, in order to tackle the infection of girls and women, it is necessary to tackle the gender inequalities that make them extremely vulnerable to infection; this may imply promoting programmes for economic empowerment, education, and promotion of rights of girls and women, as well as working on the role of men in society.

This imperative for structural changes necessitates action on several fronts. These include addressing the pervasive gender inequalities still widespread on the continent, the lack of minimum health services to detect and treat other sexual infections, and the lack of development and employment opportunities for youth as well as for the population of working age at large. This set of policies requires that changes also take place at the institutional level. Making health services youth-friendly for example, or ensuring women's access to education, is fundamental to a serious prevention strategy.

A main barrier is the lack of access to prevention experienced by a large proportion of the population on the African continent. In 2004, it was estimated that fewer than one in five people had access to HIV prevention services. There were also only around three condoms per year available for each person of sexually active age in Africa. This is clearly insufficient. Substantial resources need to be mobilized to close the 'prevention access gap'. The resource gap between the estimated funds available for prevention in sub-Saharan Africa, $421 million, and the need, $1.9 billion, is a staggering $1.48 billion (Global HIV Prevention Working Group, 2003).

Availability of Treatment

Opportunities By restoring health and prolonging life, treatment for AIDS benefits not only those who are ill, but also their families, community and the nation in which they live. As individual nations benefit, so does the rest of the continent, from the goods they produce to the services they offer and the cultural contribution they make to humanity. Furthermore, access to treatment is not simply an abstract question of logistics and economics. Each individual denied treatment is denied his or her right to life, hope and a focus on the future, laid down in Human Rights Conventions. Access to HIV/AIDS-related treatment is recognized as an integral part of fulfilling the right to health.[2]

Yet, until recently, the option of treatment for the majority of people living with HIV/AIDS in Africa had seemed impossible: high costs, demanding treatment regimes and the lack of even basic health infrastructure in many heavily affected countries were all cited as potential insurmountable barriers. A number of recent developments, however, such as the emergence of a simpler treatment regime and the dramatic drop in the price of the medication, open up opportunities for treatment provision in resource-limited settings. The WHO in 2002 also launched its ambitious '3 by 5' initiative, a major effort to scale up treatment access in resource-limited settings.

Progress in scaling up has, however, not kept pace with rising demands. Presently, the WHO estimates that there are 100,000 people on treatment in Africa – only 2 per cent of the approximately 4,400,000 people estimated to be in immediate need of treatment (WHO/UNAIDS, 2004). While more and more countries have ambitious plans for scaling up, most fall far short of reaching their targets of treating even half of those in need.

Challenges Many challenges remain in the way of scaling up AIDS treatment within African contexts. First, there are challenges related to the limited capacity of health systems. These include the low and declining number of health professionals, high drug prices, inadequate laboratory and patient care infrastructure, poor patient follow-up and weak sustainability of drug supply.

Second, there are challenges related to lack of financial resources. In 2007, it is estimated that around $3 billion will be required to meet the need for treatment in Africa. Although resources are projected to increase, they will fall far short of meeting the need (UNAIDS Global Resource Tracking Consortium, 2004). A related challenge is to sustain the level of resources that are available. The main increase in funding is projected to come from bilateral donors. Regardless of the source, all donor money is pledged for a limited amount of time. Once patients have started treatment, it must not be interrupted. If and when the donor money dries up, individual countries may not be able to foot the bill for the initiated treatment programmes.

Third, scaling up treatment also requires fostering stake-holder buy-in on all fronts – involvement by the private sector, NGOs, faith-based organizations and communities – as well as ensuring equitable access to treatment and care and overcoming stigma. A major challenge is therefore to assist African policy makers in implementing appropriate and sustainable programmes to help treat the millions of Africans already living with HIV/AIDS.

Concluding Remarks

The HIV epidemic has its origins in African poverty, and unless and until poverty is reduced there will be little progress either with reducing transmission of the virus or in an enhanced capacity to cope with its socio-economic consequences. It follows that sustained human development is essential for any effective response to the epidemic in Africa. This is a conclusion that has yet to permeate approaches to the epidemic not only in Africa but more or less everywhere. While the HIV epidemic makes sustained human development more and more unattainable, and actually adds to poverty, it also destroys the human resource capacities essential for an effective response.

The characteristics of the poor are well known, as also are some of the causal factors at work which contribute to a 'culture of poverty' – the fact that the children of the poor often become the poor of succeeding generations. Poverty is associated with weak endowments of human and financial resources, such as low levels of education with associated low levels of literacy and few marketable skills, generally poor health status and low labour productivity as a result. An aspect of the low health status of the poor is the existence amongst many Africans of undiagnosed and untreated STDs, which is now recognized as a very significant co-factor in the transmission of HIV. Poor households typically have few if any financial or other assets and are often politically and socially marginalized. These conditions of social exclusion increase the problems of reaching these populations through programmes aimed at changing sexual and other behaviours.

It is not at all surprising in these circumstances that the poor adopt behaviours which expose them to HIV infection. It is not simply that prevention activities are unlikely to reach the poor (which is too often the case) but also that such messages are often irrelevant and inoperable given the reality of their lives. Even if the poor understand what they are being urged to do, they rarely have either the incentive or the resources to adopt the recommended behaviours. Indeed, to take the long view in sexual or other behaviours is antithetical to the condition of being poor. For the poor it is the here and now that matters, and policies and programmes that recommend deferral of gratification will, and do, fall on deaf ears. Even more fundamental to the condition of poverty is social and political exclusion. So HIV-specific programmes are neglectful of the interests of the poor and are rarely if ever related to their needs, and so also, unfortunately, are other non-HIV-related programme activities – such as those relating to agriculture and credit. More generally it is the absence of effective programmes aimed at sustainable livelihoods which limits the possibilities of changing the socioeconomic conditions of the poor. But unless the reality of the lives of the poor is changed, they will persist with behaviours which expose them to HIV infection (and all the consequences of this for themselves and their families).

Herein lies the problem: how to achieve the sustainable development essential for an effective response to the epidemic under conditions where the epidemic is destructive of the capacities essential for the response. Simple answers to this problem do not exist, but at least recognition of its existence is a step towards its solution. The next step has to be the development of policies and programmes that address the inter-relationships between poverty and development and actually to put in place those activities that can make a difference for development outcomes. Central to these activities are programmes that address poverty today so as to facilitate socio-economic development tomorrow. For unless the intergenerational effects of HIV are addressed now, it is optimistic in the extreme to assume that Africa will become a pole of development in succeeding decades.

The policy implications of understanding the broader causes of the AIDS epidemic in Africa are reason for both optimism and pessimism. Reducing HIV transmission requires health education, availability of condoms and also a broad assault on malnutrition, diarrhoeal diseases and parasitic diseases, including malaria and schistosomiasis. To treat those already infected will require upgrading the health services infrastructure and expanding health education. The steps that are necessary for both prevention and treatment of HIV/AIDS are the same as for addressing the other health and development needs of poor countries. Identifying those needs is relatively easy, but they have not been adequately addressed in the past – not by the governments of poor countries or by their bilateral and multilateral aid partners.

The response to AIDS has now reached a critical turning point. For the millions of people living with HIV/AIDS, the promises of increased access to prevention and treatment services remain unfulfilled. To transform their hope into reality, an unprecedented expansion of prevention, treatment and care services will have to take place in most African countries. This is a substantial challenge as it involves reversing several decades of low investment in the public sector, particularly in health.

Glossary

Acquired Not inherited from the gene from one's parent but derived from the environment.

AIDS Acquired Immune Deficiency Syndrome, which means that the body loses the ability to fight infections because the immune system is weakened by HIV.

AIDS-related disease or HIV-related disease Symptoms caused by HIV infection that do not necessarily indicate full AIDS; e.g. swollen lymph glands, long-lasting diarrhoea, fever, tiredness. The term may also be used for full AIDS.

Antiretrovirals (ARVs) Drugs that fight retroviruses such as HIV.

Clinical Observable disease symptoms, medical.

Epidemic An unusual marked increase in cases in a fairly short period of time.

HIV negative Having no antibodies to HIV; this usually means that no HIV is present.

HIV positive Having antibodies to HIV in the blood and therefore having HIV infections.

Immune system The body's defence mechanism to fight against infections and cancer, as well as complex cellular responses in the lymph and blood; HIV primarily affects all mediated immunity.

Incidence New cases of infection in a population within a fixed period (usually a year).

Opportunistic infection (OI) Infection by an organism that only causes disease when the immune system is weak, as in advanced HIV infection.

Pandemic A global or very widespread epidemic.

Prevalence The level of existing infection in a population at a point in time, regardless of when the infection occurred.

Retrovirus Unusual, recently identified group of viruses, including HIV, which reproduces in a different way from most other viruses.

Tuberculosis (TB) Serious, chronic bacterial disease of the lungs and sometimes other organs; common with AIDS. TB is treatable with various antibiotics, although multi-drug-resistant TB is an increasing problem worldwide.

Notes

Chapter 1   Stagnation, Decline and Vulnerability: A Brief History of Post-colonial Africa

1   The enhanced HIPC stipulates that in order to qualify for relief, a country must have a debt/exports ratio of 150 per cent and debt/tax ratio of 250 per cent or more combined with tax/GDP and exports/GDP ratios of at least 15 per cent and 30 per cent.
2   Statement of the Development GAP on the proposed multilateral and G-7 Debt-reduction Plan (October 1999).
3   Government of Zambia, 'Zambian Proposal to Accelerate the National Response to HIV/AIDS through a Multi-Donor Debt Relief Programme', draft proposal as of 16 September 1999.

Chapter 4   The Challenge of Scaling Up HIV/AIDS Treatment Programmes in Africa

1   For a review of technical issues relating to ART see WHO (2002b). An excellent review of current issues is to be found in DFID/WHO (2003).
2   See, for example, Katzenstein et al. (2003). See also the discussion below on the Médecins sans Frontières and government of South Africa pilot project in Khayelitsha, where the involvement of the community has been central to the provision of ART.

3 'Structured treatment interruption' is where people who have been taking anti-HIV treatment and have chronic infection may take breaks from this treatment.
4 This review of Botswana draws heavily on a presentation by M. Markowitz and P. Wilson (2003). See also UNAIDS (2003).

Chapter 6   Setting Priorities for Confronting HIV/AIDS in Africa

1 *http://www.theglobalfund.org/en/files/pledges&contributions.xls*, accessed 27 May 2005.
2 See General Comment 14, UN Human Rights Committee.

References

ADB (2003). African Development Report (1994–1996). Abidjan, Côte d'Ivoire.

Ainsworth, M. and I. Semali (1995). The Impact of Adult Deaths on Household Composition. Mimeo. World Bank, Washington, DC.

Arndt, C. (2002). HIV/AIDS and Macroeconomic Prospects for Mozambique: An Initial Assessment. Purdue University, Indiana, Center for Global Trade Analysis.

Arndt, C. and S. Lewis (2000). 'The Macro Implications of HIV/AIDS in South Africa: A Preliminary Assessment'. *South African Journal of Economics* 68(5): 1–32.

Badcock-Walters, P., C. Desmond and W. Heard (2003). Educator Mortality In-Service in KwaZulu Natal: A Consolidated Study of HIV/AIDS Impact and Trends. Demographic and Socio-economic Conference, Durban.

Baggaley, R., P. Godfrey-Fausset, R. Msiska, D. Chilangwa, E. Chitu, J. Porter and M. Kelley (1994). 'Impact of HIV on Zambian Business'. *British Medical Journal* 309: 1549–50.

Barnett, T. and P. Blaikie (1992). *AIDS in Africa: Its Present and Future Impact.* London: Wiley and Guilford Press.

Béchu, N. (1998). 'The Impact of AIDS on the Economy of Families in Côte d'Ivoire: Changes in Consumption among AIDS-Affected Households', in M. Ainsworth, L. Fransen and M. Over (eds), *Confronting AIDS: Evidence from the Developing World.* Brussels: EU.

Bell, C., S. Devarajan and H. Gersbach (2003). Thinking About the Long-Run Economic Cost of AIDS: Theory and Application to South Africa. Policy Research Working Paper No. 3152. World Bank, Washington, DC.

BIDPA (2000). Macro-economic Impact of HIV/AIDS on Botswana. BIDPA, Gaborone.

Bond, V. and S. Wallman (1993). Report on the 1991 Survey of Households in Chiawa: Community Capacity to Prevent, Manage and Survive HIV/AIDS. *IHCAR/Hull/IAS*. Hull, University of Hull.

Bonnel, R. (2000). 'HIV/AIDS and Economic Growth: A Global Perspective'. *Journal of South African Economics* 68(5): 820–55.

Booysen, F. le R. and M. Bachmann (2002). HIV/AIDS, Poverty and Growth: Evidence from a Household Impact Study conducted in the Free State Province, South Africa. Annual Conference of the Centre for the Study of African Economies, 18–19 March, St Catherine's College, Oxford.

Burr, T., J. Hyman and G. Myers (2001). 'The Origin of Acquired Immune Deficiency Syndrome: Darwinian or Lamarckian?' *Philosophical Transactions of the Royal Society of London* B(356): 877–87.

Caldwell, J. (1995). 'Understanding the AIDS Epidemic and Reacting Sensibly to It'. *Social Science and Medicine* 41(3): 299–302.

Caldwell, J., P. Caldwell, E. Maxine Ankrah, John K. Anarfi, Dominic K. Agyeman, Kofi Awusabo-Asare and I. Orubuloye (1993). 'African Families and AIDS: Context, Reactions and Potential Intervention'. *Health Transition Review* 3(Supplement): 1–16.

Caldwell, J., I. Orubuloye and P. Caldwell (2000). 'Male and Female Circumcision in Africa: From a Regional to a Specific Nigerian Examination', in J. Caldwell, P. Caldwell and I. Orubuloye (eds), *Towards the Containment of the AIDS Epidemic: Social and Behavioural Research*. Canberra: Health Transition Center, Australian National University.

Callaghy, T. M. (1991). 'Africa and the World Economy: Caught between a Rock and a Hard Place', in J. W. Harbeson and D. Rothchild (eds), *Africa in World Politics*. Boulder, CO: Westview Press.

Centre for AIDS Development, Research and Evaluation-Cadre (2002). Integrated Community-Based Home Care (ICHC) in South Africa: A Review of the Model Implemented by the

Hospice Association of South Africa. Policy project, Cape Town.

Cheru, F. (2002). *African Renaissance: Roadmaps to the Challenge of Globalization*. London and New York: Zed Books.

CHGA (2003). The AIDS Epidemic. United Nations Commission on HIV/AIDS and Governance in Africa, Addis Ababa.

CHGA (2004a). HIV/AIDS and Rural Communities. United Nations Commission on HIV/AIDS and Governance in Africa, Addis Ababa.

CHGA (2004b). Impact of HIV/AIDS on Gender, Orphans and Vulnerable Children. Discussion Outcomes of CHGA Interactive Cameroon. United Nations Commission on HIV/AIDS and Governance in Africa, Addis Ababa.

CHGA (2004c). Impact of HIV/AIDS on Government Departments. United Nations Commission on HIV/AIDS and Governance in Africa, Addis Ababa.

CHGA (2004d). Mozambique: The Challenge of AIDS Treatment and Care. United Nations Commission on HIV/AIDS and Governance in Africa, Addis Ababa.

CHGA (2005). AIDS and Children in Africa. United Nations Commission on HIV/AIDS and Governance in Africa, Addis Ababa.

Chossudovsky, M. (1994). 'Global Impoverishment and the IMF-World Bank: Economic Medicine'. *Third World Resurgence* 49: 20.

Chronic Poverty Research Centre (2004). *The Chronic Poverty Report 2004–5*. Manchester: CPRC.

Cogneau, D. and M. Grimm (2002). *AIDS and Income Distribution in Africa: A Micro-simulation Study for Côte d'Ivoire*. Paris: Dial.

Cohen, D. (2002). Human Capital and the HIV Epidemic in Sub-Saharan Africa. ILO Programme on HIV/AIDS and the World of Work, Geneva.

Commission on Macroeconomics and Health (2004). Chronic Poverty, Health and HIV/AIDS. Draft paper. WHO, Geneva.

Cribb, J. (2001). 'The Origin of Acquired Immune Deficiency Syndrome: Can Science Afford to Ignore It?' *Philosophical Transactions of the Royal Society of London* B(356): 935–8.

Cuddington, J. T. (1993). 'Modeling the Macroeconomic Effects of AIDS with an Application to Tanzania'. *World Bank Economic Review* 7(2): 173–89.

Cuddington, J. T. and J. D. Hancock (1994). 'Assessing the Impact of AIDS on the Growth Path of the Malawian Economy'. *Journal of Development Economics* 43(2): 363–8.

Cullinan, K. (2000). Memory Boxes. Health e-News Service (29 September). *http://www.health-e.org.za/news/article.php?uid= 20000927*

Cullinan, K. (2003). Health Sector Feels AIDS Impact. Health Systems Trust, Durban.

Darkoh, E. (2005). *Provision of Large-Scale Antiretroviral Therapy in Africa: Applying Lessons Learned in Botswana*. CHGA Interactive: Addressing the Socio-economic Impacts of AIDS in Africa. Economic Commission for Africa, Casablanca, Morocco.

Decosas, J. and A. Adrien (1997). 'Migration and AIDS'. *AIDS* 11(Supplement A): S77–84.

Desmond, C. and J. Gow (2001). 'Sickness, Death and Poverty – Our Bequest to Orphans'. *Children First* 6(40): 19–24.

Desmond, C., K. Michael and J. Gow (2000). The Hidden Battle: HIV/AIDS in the Family and Community. Health Economics & HIV/AIDS Research Division, Durban, University of Natal.

DFID/WHO (2003). Provision of Antiretroviral Therapy in Resource-Limited Settings: A Review of Experience up to August 2003 (November).

Donahue, J. (1998). Community-Based Economic Support for Households Affected by HIV/AIDS. Washington, DC: USAID HIV/AIDS Division.

Drimie, S. (2002). The Impact of HIV/AIDS on Land: Case Studies from Kenya, Lesotho and South Africa. Human Sciences Research Council, Pretoria.

Drinkwater, M. (1993). The Effects of HIV/AIDS on Agricultural Production Systems in Zambia. FAO, Rome.

Engh, I., L. Stloukal and J. du Guerny (2000). HIV/AIDS in Namibia: The Impact on the Livestock Sector. FAO, Rome.

EURODAD (1999). Towards a Comprehensive Solution to the Debt Problem. Contribution towards the HIPC Review, Phase II (August). Brussels.

FAO Committee on World Food Security (2001). *The Impact of HIV/AIDS on Food Security*. Twenty-Seventh Session, Rome.

Farmer, P. (1999). *Infections and Inequalities: The Modern Plagues*. Berkeley: University of California Press.

Farmer, P., M. Connors and J. Simmons (eds) (1996). *Women, Poverty and AIDS: Sex, Drugs and Structural Violence*. Monroe, ME: Common Courage Press.

Fylknes, K., A. Haworth, C. Rosenvard and P. Kwapa (1999). 'HIV Counselling and Testing: Overemphasising High Acceptance Rates a Threat to Confidentiality and the Right Not to Know'. *AIDS* 13: 2469–74.

Gauteng Health Department in South Africa (2002). Report of the Public Service AIDS Indaba. Misty Hills, Gauteng.

Geffen, N., N. Natrass and C. Raubenheimer (2003). The Cost of HIV Prevention and Treatment Interventions in South Africa. CSSR Working Paper No. 28. Centre for Social Research, University of Cape Town, South Africa.

Gilks, C. (1998). Sexual Health and Health Care: Care and Support for People with HIV/AIDS in Resource-Poor Settings. Department for International Development, London.

Global HIV Prevention Working Group (2003). Access to HIV Prevention: Closing the Gap. Seattle: Bill and Melinda Gates Foundation/Henry J. Kaiser Family Foundation.

Goyer, K. (2001). 'HIV and Political Instability in Sub-Saharan Africa'. *AIDS Analysis Africa* 12(1): 13, 16.

Greener, R. (2000). Impacts of HIV/AIDS on Poverty and Income Inequality in Botswana. Botswana Institute for Development Policy Analysis, Gaborone.

Greener, R., K. Jefferis and H. Siphambe (2000). 'The Impact of HIV/AIDS on Poverty and Inequality in Botswana'. *South African Journal of Economics* 68(5): 888–915.

Hansen-Kuhn, K. and S. Hellinger (1999). 'SAPs Link Sharpens Debt-Relief Debate'. *Third World Network*, July. *http://www.twnside.org.sg/title/1926-cn.htm*

Hope, K. R. (2001). 'Africa's HIV/AIDS Crisis in Development Context'. *International Relations* 15(6): 15–36.

Hope, S. and S. Gaborone (1999). HIV/AIDS and Mobile Population Groups in Botswana. Government of Botswana, Gaborone.

Horowitz, L. (1996). *Emerging Viruses: AIDS and Ebola – Nature, Accident or Intentional?* Sandpoint, ID: Tetrahedron Press.

Hosegood, V., K. Herbst and I. Timæus (2003). The Impact of Adult AIDS Deaths on Households and Children's Living Arrangements in Rural South Africa. Conference on the Empirical Evidence for the Demographic and Socio-economic Impact of AIDS, Durban.

Huddart, J., R. Furth and J. V. Lyons (2004). The Zambia HIV/AIDS Workforce Study: Preparing for Scale-Up. Quality Assurance Project, Bethesda, MD.

IMF (1989). IMF: World Economic Outlook. Data file.

IMF (200.). IMF: International Financial Statistics.

INE (2002). Impacto Demográfico do HIV/SIDA em Moçambique. MISAU.

IRIN (2003). BOTSWANA: More than Money Needed for Successful AIDS Programme. Press release (4 August).

Jakab, E. A. M. (2000). *Louis Pasteur: Hunting Killer Germs.* London: McGraw-Hill.

Kaleeba, N. (2001). From Despair to Hope: Home and Community Care for Persons Living with or Affected by HIV/AIDS in Africa. 1st SADC Conference on Community Home-Based Care, Gaborone, Botswana.

Kaleeba, N., S. Kalibala, M. Kaseje, P. Ssebbanja, S. Anderson, E. van Praag, G. Tembo and E. Katabira (1997). 'Participatory Evaluation of Counselling, Medical and Social Services of The AIDS Support Organization (TASO) in Uganda'. *AIDS Care* 9(1): 13–26.

Kaliyati, J., N. Madzingira, Z. Jokomo, M. Francis-Chizorono and R. M. Kaliyati (2003). HIV/AIDS and Child Labour in Zimbabwe: A Rapid Assessment. Paper no 2. ILO/IPEC, Geneva and Harare, and Institute of Development Studies, University of Zimbabwe.

Kambou, G., S. Devarajan and M. Over (1992). 'The Economic Impact of AIDS in an African Country: Simulations with a Computable General Equilibrium Model of Cameroon'. *Journal of African Economies* 1(1): 109–30.

Katzenstein, D., M. Laga and J. P. Moatti (2003). 'The Evaluation of HIV/AIDS Drug Access Initiatives in Côte D'Ivoire, Senegal and Uganda: How Access to Antiretroviral Treatment Can Become Feasible in Africa'. *AIDS* 17(3): S1–4.

Kelly, K. (2001). Bambisanani: Community Orientation to HIV/AIDS Prevention, Care and Support. Centre for AIDS Development, Johannesburg, South Africa, Research and Evaluation.

Kenyan Ministry of Health (2002). National Home-Based Care Policy Guidelines. Kenyan Ministry of Health, Nairobi.

Kim, J. Y., J. V. Millen and A. Irwin (eds) (2000). *Dying for Growth: Global Inequality and the Health of the Poor.* Monroe, ME: Common Courage Press.

Konde-Lule, J., R. Ssengonzi, R. McNamara, C. Li, M. Wawer, J. Edmondson and R. Kelly (1993). HIV-Related Mortality and Household Economic Burden. Rakai, Uganda.

Kwaramba, P. (1997). The Socio-economic Impact of HIV/AIDS on Communal Agricultural Production Systems in Zimbabwe. Zimbabwe Farmers' Union and Friedrich Ebert Stiftung, Harare.

Lipumba, N. (1994). Africa Beyond Adjustment. Overseas Development Council, Washington, DC.

Los Alamos National Laboratory (2005). The Circulating Recombinant Forms. *http://www.hiv.lanl.gov/content/hiv-db/CRFs/CRFs.html*

Lundberg, M., P. Mujinja and M. Over (2000). Sources of Financial Assistance for Households Suffering an Adult Death in Kagera, Tanzania. World Bank, Washington, DC.

Lurie, M., B. Williams, K. Zuma, D. Myaka-Mwamburi, G. P. Garnett, M. Sweat, J. Gittelsohn and S. S. A. Karim (2003). 'Who Infects Whom? HIV-1 Concordance and Discordance among Migrant and Non-Migrant Couples in South Africa'. *AIDS* 17(15): 2245–52.

Machipisa, L. (2001). Women and Girls Carry the Heaviest Burden. *http://www.ipsnews.net/hivaids/section1_3.shtml*

McNeill, W. H. (1998). *Plagues and Peoples*. New York: Anchor.

Maizels, A. (1995). 'The Functioning of International Markets for Primary Commodities: Key Policy Issues for Developing Countries'. *International Monetary and Financial Issues for the 1990s* V.

Malawi Institute of Management (2002). The Impact of HIV/AIDS on Human Resources in the Public Sector of Malawi (unpublished).

Mann, J. M. (1999). 'Medicine and Public Health, Ethics and Human Rights', in J. M. Mann, S. Gruskin, M. A. Grodin and G. J. Annas (eds), *Health and Human Rights: A Reader*. London: Routledge.

Mann, J. and D. Tarantola (eds) (1992). *AIDS in the World*. Cambridge, MA: Harvard University Press.

Markowitz, M. and P. Wilson (2003). The Botswana National ARV Program. Millennium Project HIV/AIDS Task Force.

Mbilinyi, M. and N. Kaihula (2000). 'Sinners and Outsiders: The Drama of AIDS in Rungwe', in C. Baylies and J. Bujira (eds),

AIDS, Sexuality and Gender in Africa: Collective Strategies and Struggles in Tanzania and Zambia. London: Routledge.

MEDILINKS (2001). African Statistics: Cost of HIV/AIDS, Malaria & TB to Africa. *http://www.medilinkz.org/healthtopics/statistics/Statistics%20in%20Africa%2002001.htm*

Ministério da Saúde (2003a). Relatorio de Avaliação Conjunta (Joint Annual Evaluation). Mozambique.

Ministério da Saúde (2003b). PEN ITS/HIV/SIDA – Sector Saúde 2004–2008. Mozambique.

Morar, N. S., G. Ramjee and S. S. A. Karim (1998). Safe Sex Practices among Sex Workers at Risk of HIV Infection. UNAIDS, Geneva.

Mutangadura, G. B. (2000). Household Welfare Impacts of Mortality of Adult Females in Zimbabwe: Implications for Policy and Program Development. AIDS and Economics Symposium, Durban, South Africa.

Mutangadura, G. and D. Webb (1999). Mortality and Morbidity on Households in Kafue District, Zambia. SAFAIDS, Harare.

Nabwire, J. (2000). The Uganda Memory Project: Mothers Disclosing Their HIV Status to Their Children. KIT, Kampala. *http://www.kit.nl/frameset.asp?/ils/exchange_content/html/2000_1_uganda_memory_project.asp&frnr=1&*

Namposya-Serpell, N. (2000). Social and Economic Risk Factors for HIV/AIDS-Affected Families in Zambia. AIDS and Economics Symposium, IAEN, 7–8 July, Durban, South Africa.

Nandakumar, A., P. Schneider and D. Butera (2000). *Use of and Expenditures on Outpatient Health Care by a Group of HIV Positive Individuals in Rwanda*. Bethesda, MD: Abt Associates Inc.

Niyongabo, C. (2001). Impact of HIV/AIDS on Poor Urban Livelihoods. Presentation for Save the Children UK, Gitega, Burundi.

Odipo, G. (2000). Adolescent AIDS Epidemic in Kenya: Lessons from Child Abuse Proportion. East Cape Training Centre, Port Elizabeth, South Africa.

Orubuloye, I. and J. Caldwell (1997). 'Perceived Male Sexual Needs and Male Sexual Behaviour in Southwest Nigeria'. *Social Science and Medicine* 44(8): 1195–207.

Orubuloye, I., J. Caldwell and P. Caldwell (1993). 'African Women's Control Over Their Sexuality in an Era of AIDS'. *Social Science and Medicine* 37(7): 859–72.

Over, M. (1992). The Macro-economic Impact of AIDS in Africa. Technical Working Paper No. 3. Washington, DC: World Bank.

Parfitt, T. and S. Riley (1989). *The African Debt Crisis*. London: Routledge.

Poku, N. K. (2001). 'Africa's AIDS Crisis in Context: How the Poor are Dying'. *Third World Quarterly* 22: 191–204.

Poku, N. K. and A. Whiteside (eds) (2004). *The Political Economy of AIDS in Africa*. Aldershot: Ashgate.

Rau, B. (2003). HIV/AIDS and Child Labour: A State-of-the-art Review. IPEC paper no. 6. International Labour Organization, Geneva.

Rugalema, G. (1998). It is Not Only the Loss of Labour: HIV/AIDS, Loss of Household Assets and Household Livelihood in Bukoba District, Tanzania. East and Southern Africa Regional Conference on Responding to HIV/AIDS: Development Needs of African Smallholder Agriculture, Harare, Zimbabwe.

Sachs, J. D. (2001). Macroeconomics and Health: Investing in Health for Economic Development. Presented to Gro Harlem Brundtland, Director-General of the World Health Organization (20 December).

SAFAIDS/CFU (1996). Orphans on Farms: Who Cares? An Exploratory Study into Fostering Orphaned Children on Commercial Farms in Zimbabwe. Southern Africa AIDS Information Dissemination Service/Commercial Farmers Union, Harare.

Save the Children UK (2002). Household Economy Assessment (Nyaminyami) Kariba Rural District, Mashonaland West Province, Zimbabwe (unpublished).

Schoepf, B. (1993). 'AIDS Action-Research with Women in Kinshasa, Zaïre'. *Social Science and Medicine* 37(11): 1401–13.

Schubert, B. (2003). Social Welfare Interventions for AIDS-Affected Households in Zambia. GTZ (German Technical Co-operation), Lusaka, Zambia.

Semkiwa, H., J. Tweve, A. Mnenge, Y. Mwaituka, H. Mlawa and E. Kawala (2003). HIV/AIDS and Child Labour in the United Republic of Tanzania: A Rapid Assessment – A Case Study of Dar es Salaam and Arusha. Paper No. 3. International Labour Organization, Geneva.

Silomba, W. (2002). 'HIV/AIDS and Development – the Chikankata Experience', in *One Step Further – Responses to HIV/AIDS, SIDA Studies* 7. Swedish International Development Cooperation Agency, Stockholm.

Simmons, J., P. Farmer and B. G. Schoepf (1996). 'A Global Perspective', in P. Farmer, M. Connors and J. Simmons (eds), *Women, Poverty and AIDS: Sex, Drugs and Structural Violence*. Monroe, ME: Common Courage Press.

Steinberg, M., S. Johnson, G. Scierhout and D. Ndegwa (2002). Hitting Home: How Households Cope with the Impact of the HIV/AIDS Epidemic: A Survey of Households Affected by HIV/AIDS in South Africa. Henry J. Kaiser Family Foundation and the Health Systems Trust, Washington, DC.

Stillwagon, E. (2001). 'AIDS and Poverty in Africa'. *The Nation*, 21 May.

Swaziland, Government of (2002). Assessment of the Impact of HIV/AIDS on the Central Agencies of the Government of the Kingdom of Swaziland: Executive Summary. Government of Swaziland, Mbabane.

Tibaijuka, A. K. (1997). 'AIDS and Economic Welfare in Peasant Agriculture: Case Studies from Kagabiro Village, Kagera Region, Tanzania'. *World Development* 25: 963–75.

Topouzis, D. (1994). Uganda – The Socio-economic Impact of HIV/AIDS on Rural Families with an Emphasis on Youth. FAO, Rome.

Topouzis, D. (2000). Measuring the Impact of HIV/AIDS on the Agricultural Sector in Africa. African Development Forum, Addis Ababa, Ethiopia.

Tumushabe, J. (2003). Situational Analysis of AIDS-Induced Child Labour in Uganda and Experience of Community Empowerment to Manage the Crisis. ILO/IPEC Technical Workshop on HIV/AIDS and Child Labour, Lusaka, Zambia.

Ugandan Ministry of Agriculture, Animal Industry and Fisheries (2002). The Impact of HIV/AIDS on Agricultural Production and Mainstreaming HIV/AIDS Messages into Agricultural Extension in Uganda. FAO, Rome.

UN/DESA (2005a). The Impact of AIDS. United Nations, New York.

UN/DESA (2005b). World Population Prospects. The 2004 Revision. Highlights. United Nations, New York.

UNAIDS (1999). A Review of Household and Community Responses to the HIV/AIDS Epidemic in the Rural Areas of Sub-Saharan Africa. UNAIDS, Geneva.

UNAIDS (2002). Report on the Global HIV/AIDS Epidemic. UNAIDS, Geneva.

UNAIDS (2003). Stepping Back from the Edge: The Pursuit of Antiretroviral Therapy in Botswana, South Africa and Uganda. UNAIDS Best Practice Collection. UNAIDS, Geneva (November).

UNAIDS (2004a). AIDS Epidemic Update. UNAIDS, Geneva.

UNAIDS (2004b). Report on the Global AIDS Epidemic. UNAIDS, Geneva.

UNAIDS/World Bank/GFATM (2004). 'Three Ones': Key Principles. UNAIDS, Geneva.

UNAIDS Global Resource Tracking Consortium (2004). Financing the Expanded Response to AIDS. UNAIDS, Geneva.

UNCTAD (1999). The Least Developed Countries 1999 Report. UNCTAD, Geneva.

UNCTAD (2002). The Least Developed Countries 2002 Report. UNCTAD, Geneva.

UNDP (2000). Botswana Human Development Report 2000. UNDP, Gaborone, Botswana.

UNDP (2001). Human Development Report 2001, Burkina Faso. UNDP, Ouagadougou, Burkina Faso.

UNDP (2002). *Human Development Report.* Oxford: Oxford University Press.

UNDP (2004). *Human Development Report.* Oxford: Oxford University Press.

UNECA (2000). *HIV/AIDS and Economic Development in Sub-Saharan Africa.* Addis Ababa: African Development Forum, United Nations Economic Commission for Africa.

Unger, A., T. Welz and D. Haran (2002). The Impact of HIV/AIDS on Health Care Staff at a Rural South African Hospital, 1990–2001. London School of Hygiene and Tropical Medicine/University of California, San Francisco.

UNICEF (1987). *Adjustment with a Human Face.* New York: UNICEF.

UNICEF (1998). Orphan Programming in Zambia: Developing a Strategy for Very Young Children in Zambia (draft). UNICEF, Lusaka, Zambia.

UNICEF/UNAIDS/USAID (2004). Children on the Brink 2004. A Joint Report of New Orphans Estimates and a Framework for Action. New York: UNICEF.

Waller, K. (1998). The Impact of HIV/AIDS on Farming Households in the Monze District of Zambia. University of Bath, UK.

Whiteside, A. (2002). 'Poverty and HIV/AIDS in Africa'. *Third World Quarterly* 23(2): 313–32.

Whiteside, A. and C. Sunter (2000). *AIDS: The Challenge for South Africa*. Cape Town: Human & Rousseau Tafelberg.

WHO (2000). Health: A Precious Asset. Accelerating Follow-up to the World Summit for Social Development. WHO, Geneva.

WHO (2002a). Impact of AIDS on Older People in Africa: Zimbabwe Case Study. WHO, Geneva.

WHO (2002b). Scaling up ART in Resource-Limited Settings: Guidelines for a Public Health Approach. WHO, Geneva.

WHO (2003). Antiretroviral Therapy in Primary Health Care: Experience of the Khayelitsha Programme in South Africa. WHO, Geneva.

WHO (2004). Draft Paper on Chronic Poverty, Health and HIV/AIDS. Geneva, WHO.

WHO/UNAIDS (2004). 3 by 5 Progress Report, December 2003 through June 2004. WHO, Geneva.

WHO/UNAIDS/International AIDS Society (2004). Safe and Effective Use of Antiretroviral Treatments in Adults, with Particular Reference to Resource-Limited Settings. WHO, Geneva.

WHO-AFRO (2003). HIV/AIDS Epidemiological Surveillance Update for the WHO African Region 2002. World Health Organization, Regional Office for Africa, Harare.

Wilkins, C. M. (2003). Re-stabilizing Family Structures Affected by HIV/AIDS: Is There Hope? Zimbabwe Case Study. School for International Training, Brattleboro, Vermont.

Williams, B. G., D. Gilgen, C. M. Campbell, D. Taljaard and C. MacPhail (2000). *The Natural History of HIV/AIDS in South Africa: A Biomedical and Social Survey in Carletonville*. Johannesburg: Centre for Scientific and Industrial Research.

World Bank (1981). World Development Report 1981. World Bank, Washington, DC.

World Bank (1989). Sub-Saharan Africa: From Crisis to Sustainable Growth. Washington, DC.

World Bank (1990). Implementing the World Bank's Strategy to Reduce Poverty: Progress and Challenges. Washington, DC.

World Bank (1993). Adjustment in Africa: Reforms, Results and the Road Ahead. World Bank, Washington, DC.

World Bank (1994). *The Challenge of Development*. New York: Oxford University Press.

World Bank (1996). The African Capacity Building Initiative: Progress and Challenges. Washington, DC.

World Bank (1998). African Development Report. Washington, DC.

World Bank (1999). Can Africa Claim the 21st Century? World Bank, Washington, DC.

World Bank (2000a). Africa Development Indicators 2000. World Bank, Washington, DC.

World Bank (2000b). Intensifying Action Against HIV/AIDS in Africa: Responding to a Development Crisis. World Bank, Washington, DC.

World Bank (2002). Africa Development Indicators 2002. World Bank, Washington, DC.

World Bank (2003a). Global Economic Prospects 2004. World Bank, Washington, DC.

World Bank (2003b). World Development Indicators. World Bank, Washington, DC.

World Bank (2004). Africa Development Indicators 2004. World Bank, Washington, DC.

Yamano, T. and T. S. Jayne (2002). Measuring the Impacts of Prime-Age Adult Death on Rural Households in Kenya. Staff Paper 2002–26. Department of Agricultural Economics, Michigan State University, East Lansing, MI.

Zimbabwe National AIDS Council (2004). The HIV and AIDS Epidemic in Zimbabwe: Where Are We Now? Where Are We Going? Zimbabwe National AIDS Council, Harare.

'Zuki' (2003). Interview with Nana Poku. South Africa (Feb.).

Index